HARRISBURG, ARKANSAS

Birthplace and Home of Gen. George H. Thomas.

THE
Southampton Insurrection

BY

WILLIAM SIDNEY DREWRY, Ph. B., M. A.
(*University of Va.*)
HONORARY SCHOLAR IN HISTORY, JOHNS HOPKINS UNIVERSITY

Historia * * * *scribitur ad narrandum, non ad probandum*
—QUINTILIAN: *X, 1, 31*

WASHINGTON:
THE NEALE COMPANY
431 ELEVENTH STREET NORTHWEST
1900

TO
MY VALUED FRIEND AND KIND
INSTRUCTOR,
RICHARD HEATH DABNEY, M. A., PH. D.,
PROFESSOR OF HISTORY, UNIVERSITY OF VIRGINIA,
WHOSE INCITATION AND SYMPATHY HAVE
EVER INSPIRED ME,
THIS VOLUME
IS GRATEFULLY INSCRIBED.

CONTENTS.

CHAPTER I.

REVIVED IMPORTANCE OF SLAVERY—Industrial, social and political development—Revived study of economics—Virginia's progress in internal improvements and education—Improved condition of the negro, socially, politically, and intellectually.......................... 9

CHAPTER II.

THE INSURRECTION—Description of Southampton County—Its condition, social, political, and financial—The development of the plot: time chosen for arousing the slaves; character of the originator of the insurrection—The raid: from the meeting in the woods to the first resistance at Parker's Field; from Parker's Field to Nat's return to the rendezvous in the woods—Pursuit and capture of the insurgents; why the negroes were not sooner suppressed by the citizens; cause of the delay of distant militia; aid furnished by Virginia and Carolina troops; efficient service of cavalry; cases of rashness and escape of guilty negroes; reason and humanity prevail; capture of Nat Turner—Trials and executions.... 20

CHAPTER III.

RELATIONS TO SLAVERY AND THE SOUTH—Condition of the negroes of the county—System of labor such as to inspire ambition in the slave—Class system and pride—Few overseers and poor whites—Reciprocal confidence of master and servant—Great emancipation sentiment—Only one sign of rebellion previous to 1831, and this by negroes smuggled into the county—Causes of the insurrection: fanaticism and love of self-importance;

CHAPTER III.—Continued.

Inclination for robbery and plunder; influence of the St. Domingo massacre; foreign policy of the United States, (a) with South American Republics and West Indies, (b) with Mexico; Indian troubles, (a) Creeks and Cherokees, (b) Seminoles of Florida; abolition movement—General character of the insurrection—Results: its influence on slave legislation, the emancipation sentiment, and the abolition movement throughout America...... 106

CHAPTER IV.

CONCLUSION—Insurrection largely responsible for more stringent laws against negroes—Insurrections not due to cruelty of the slave system—The more sensible negroes remained loyal, while the weaker ones rebelled—Foreign influence on negro revolts—Contiguity of three bodies of free negroes to the United States—Indian troubles—Abolition movement in distant sections—Slave legislation—The negro as a free citizen...................... 181

APPENDIX.

A. List of negroes brought before the Court of Southampton. 195
B. List of white persons murdered in the Insurrection...... 196
C. Principal citizens interviewed personally............... 197
D. Bibliography 198

ILLUSTRATIONS.

Birthplace and Home of Gen. George H. Thomas	Frontispiece
Map of Southampton County	19
Site of the Residence of Mr. Joseph Travis	26
Portrait of Nat Turner	28
Nat Turner's Bible	32
Persons' Mill Pond	34
Home of Mr. Salathiel Francis	38
The Turner Farm	42
Home of Mrs. Catherine Whitehead	44
Barnes' M. E. Church	47
Home of Mr. Richard Porter	49
Home of Nathaniel Francis	50
Cuddy at Nathaniel Francis'	52
Portrait of Mrs. Lavinia Francis	54
Portrait of Hardie Musgrave	56
Site of the Home of Capt. John T. Barrow	58
Elm Growing on the Grave of Capt. J. T. Barrow	60
Capt. Newit Harris' Brandy Cellar	62
Site of Kitchen at Levi Waller's	64
Portrait of Mr. and Mrs. Wall	67
Old Shop at Waller's	69
Home of Mrs. Rebecca Vaughn	70
Blackhead Sign Post	72
Residence of Mr. James Parker	75
Parker's Gate	76
Battlefield in Parker's Field	76
Bridge Over Nottoway River at Jerusalem	78
Cypress Bridge Over Nottoway River	80
Ridley's Quarters	82
Residence of Dr. Simon Blunt	84
Turner's Methodist Church	86
Nat Turner's Cave	90
Nat Turner's Sword	92
Home of Benjamin Phipps	94
Cross Keys	96
Home of James Trezevant	98
Southampton Court House	100
Southampton Jail	102
Portrait of Mr. Collin Kitchen	102
Tree Under Which Nat Turner Was Hung	115
Place of Burial of Insurgent Negroes	115

PREFACE.

This attempt to separate truth from fiction has been exceedingly difficult, owing to the numerous misrepresentations and exaggerations which have grown up about the subject. I have studied slavery, slave legislation, and the condition of the negro in every phase that might throw light upon slave insurrections. Citizens of all classes, former slaves as well as masters, have been interviewed. The scenes of this and other insurrections have been visited in company with persons thoroughly acquainted with the country and with the facts and conditions under which they occurred. Among those interviewed were members of every family that suffered at the hands of the Southampton insurgents. Persons who had guarded the prisoners and seen them executed, relatives of Nat Turner, Hark Travis, Nelson Williams, Jeff. Edwards, and other negroes who had known the insurgents personally and labored with them, all furnished me information. These oral traditions I have endeavored to verify by comparison with each other, with official letters, proceedings of legislatures, county records, proceedings of county and superior courts, and other historical sources.

The map of Southampton county has been compiled from data in the Agricultural Handbook of Virginia and from personal investigation. I went several times carefully over the route traversed by the blacks, and, as far as possible, took note of the general directions and places in detail. Still, owing to want of adequate appliances, it was impossible to mark accurately every distance.

The thanks of the author are due to Col. Robert A. Brock, Prof. Frank P. Brent, and Mr. W. G. Stanard for valuable assistance during his researches in the Virginia State Library and the Virginia Historical Society. It is impossible to mention here the many persons, both white and colored, who, by their interest in my undertaking, have rendered it less burdensome.[1] But it is both a pleasure and a duty to acknowledge my obligations to my friends, Messrs. W. S. Francis and B. P. Woodard, who accompanied me in my journeys and rendered me distinct service in securing a better knowledge of Southampton county and the illustrations of this book. I wish also to acknowledge my indebtedness to Dr. J. C. Ballagh, of the Johns Hopkins University, for important suggestions. W. S. D.

Johns Hopkins University, January, 1900.

[1] See Appendix B.

THE SOUTHAMPTON INSURRECTION.

CHAPTER I.
REVIVED IMPORTANCE OF SLAVERY.

The third and last period into which the history of slavery in Virginia may be divided extends from 1830 to 1865. This is the period during which the nation was welded into a composite whole, the States retaining their identity, but the Union becoming *one and inseparable.* This is well illustrated in national matters, such as the Independent Treasury Act. An industrial revolution took place, fostered by an era of most important inventions, and there arose in economics and politics some of the most momentous questions which have ever confronted the United States of America. Nor was the Slave Section a laggard in the general progress. In education, politics, and industry the South took the first stand. The first steam locomotive in America was run over a short road built from Charleston to Augusta, through the rice and cotton fields of South Carolina and Georgia, while the second one started from Baltimore over the Baltimore and Ohio Railway. Both were in that section of the country where slavery existed. Also, the first message by the magnetic telegraph was sent, in 1844, from Baltimore to Washington, and this invention was the basis of the great network of submarine telegraphs which now encircle the world. The first steamer, the "Savannah," sailed across the Atlantic from Savannah, Georgia. These, together with other inventions which improved the means of communication, served to bring men closer together, and connected Europe and America more closely than

Richmond and New York had formerly been. It was a natural consequence of this development that the great importance of the United States should be so impressed upon the world that all nations desired her friendship and alliance, and, reversely, that the events of the outside world should make a marked impression on America.

The Administration of Andrew Jackson was the landmark of this period, a time of re-formation, when the spoils system was introduced permanently to demoralize politics, and when all parties forgot the good of the whole country in their sectional differences. Fully conscious of this fact, in 1835 a committee of the Senate, with Mr. Calhoun as chairman, said the spoils system was as perfect a scheme as could be desired for enlarging the power of patronage, destroying love of country, and substituting a spirit of subserviency and man-worship, encouraging vice and discouraging virtue, preparing for the subversion of liberty and the establishment of despotism. "His Presidency," says Woodrow Wilson of Jackson, "was a time of riot and of industrial revolt, of bawling turbulence in many quarters, and of disregard for law; and it has been said that the mob took its cue from the example of arbitrary temperament set them by the President."[1] For the first forty years of our National Government the ablest and most conscientious men of both parties were the candidates for office, but since 1830 the grade of men holding office, if we except Webster, Calhoun, Clay and a few others, has by no means represented the highest moral and intellectual sentiment and force of the country. Particularly was the truth of this shown by the events of the period between 1856 and 1865.[2] Through improved means of communication, material and intellectual—especially the improved postal service and

[1] Division and Reunion, p. 115.
[2] Bryce, American Commonwealth, vol. II., p. 37.

cheap newspapers—these less superior men were more easily rendered the mere puppets of a public sentiment, supported by unreflecting masses. Such false sentiment, encouraged by scheming politicians, gradually forced the country into the most useless and bloody controversy recorded in history, which was inevitable only in the absence of a broad patriotism and patience.

This new democracy was made doubly important by the fact that at the beginning of the period a property qualification for voting, both in Europe and America, had been abolished and a general tendency to universal suffrage introduced. In 1830 Charles X. of France was successfully dethroned and forced by the people, in spite of the bravery of the Royal Guards and the Swiss, to abdicate in favor of a plain and simple King of the People— Louis Philippe—who accepted a charter imposed upon him by the Deputies. How different the time of Louis XVIII., who granted a charter in 1815 apparently only as an act of grace! So, further under Louis Philippe the abolition of heredity in the peerage and of the censorship of journals were accomplished, the suffrage extended, and religious toleration procured. This awakening and revolution spread to all Europe. The aristocratic government fell in Switzerland; liberal innovations were established in Germany; Italy was violently agitated; Belgium separated from Holland; the Spanish Refugees wished to attempt a revolution in their own country, and England forced the Tories to grant the Reform Bill, so nobly advocated by William Cobbet, Francis Place, and Joseph Hume. England had already, in 1828, repealed the Corporation and the Test Acts and emancipated the Catholics. Even Africa and Asia felt the mighty wave of reform, and Mohammed Ali, the "Peter the Great" of Egypt, did much toward centralizing his government and suppressing the slave-trade. Mrs. Latimer says:

"Some thousands of the fellaheen, 'disgusted with the endless and systematic exactions of the Egyptian Government, crossed the deserts which separated Africa from Asia, and sought refuge in the territory of the Pasha of Acre.' This was in 1831, when Europe was too much interested in its own revolutions to pay much attention to the affairs of the East."[1]

Charles Greville graphically describes the state of affairs in Europe, when he says: "I never remember days like these, nor read of such,—the tenor and lively expectation that prevails, and the way in which people's minds are turned backward and forward from France to Ireland, then range exclusively from Poland to Piedmont, and fix again on the burnings, riots, and executions that are going on in England."[2]

Amidst all of this excitement the slaves were not forgotten. In 1841 the Kingdom of France recognized the right of visitation on the part of England for the repression of the slave trade, but it excited so much opposition that the Chamber forced the Ministers to cancel the treaty. In 1848, however, when the world was again aroused by another French revolution, a decree was signed emancipating the blacks in all the colonies of France. Socialistic doctrines were triumphant everywhere in Europe, and their influence upon America was but increased by the leverage of distance. Immediate contact would have aroused to opposition the "American Party." In the United States there was a general democratic upheaval, "a willful self-assertion of a masterful people which gave to the national spirit its first self-reliant expression of resolution and of consentaneous power,"[3] which exhibited its evils in the first National Conventions of 1831 and

[1] Europe in Africa in the Nineteenth Century, p. 35.
[2] E. W. Latimer, France in the Nineteenth Century, p. 35.
[3] Wilson, Division and Reunion, p. 115.

1832, the creatures of pure voluntary effort. Even the women took up the cue, and spinsters preached an inveterate crusade against the opposition of the other sex. So great was the agitation that not even the President and his Cabinet could agree with each other, and the latter, as well as the Vice-President, resigned in 1831. Everything was changing, both society and politics, and the agitation did not cease until it was all centred on slavery. The tariff had, previous to this period and at its beginning, agitated the Union, and in 1832 came near wrecking it, when Congress empowered the President to use the Army and Navy in forcing the collection of tariffs in South Carolina, in accordance with the acts of 1828 and 1832, which she had declared unconstitutional and "Null" and "Void." But the crisis was avoided by a reduction of the tariff, and henceforth the field was cleared for the discussion of the slavery question.

The unrest in this political field found its cause and counterpart in that of the social and economic. There was a general revival of the study of economics. In all parts of the United States publishing houses were established, such as the Georgetown Press; and the works of Adam Smith, Malthus, Ricardo, Carlyle, Ruskin, and of other students of social and economic conditions were issued. And now for the first time important publications of native Americans began to appear. Consequently, much of their attention was devoted to the cause of internal improvements, the sale of the public lands, and other economic questions, which dominated politics in our national history and probably did more to increase the power of the National Government than any other factors in our development. This result was largely brought about by the new States, which, possessed of the strongest democratic spirit, were eager for the undertaking of public improvements by the National Government, as, on account of their poverty and restricted revenue, they were unable to undertake them on an extended scale without incurring a public debt. Jefferson and others had advanced like views, but were successfully opposed until 1823, when the first appropriation for harbor improvements was passed.[1] Jackson checked the movement, but the work was continued by distributing to the States surplus revenue for this purpose. In this period then was begun a work both by the national and State governments which resulted in great material advancement in the expansion of both agriculture and commerce.

The method of State initiative in these matters was more in accord with the States' Rights principles to which Virginia and the South remained firmly attached. Though violently agitated by the slavery question, Virginia still made rapid industrial, social and literary progress, and was in the foremost rank of the States in internal development. She violently opposed the measures of the President in the Nullification Controversy, and her distinguished son, John Randolph, the representative of Virginia sentiment, bitterly denounced the Administration. With her strong conservatism, she finally assumed the position of pacificator, and sent Benjamin Watkins Leigh, one of her most renowned citizens, as a commissioner to South Carolina. The Virginia Commonwealth stood for peace at home and abroad, and no internal dissensions disturbed her own society. Her agriculture was flourishing and internal improvements were advancing on every hand.[2]

[1] Federalist (Ford's Edition), p. 280.

[2] At the head of the movement for improvements was a president and directors of public works. The report of the Public Engineer to this board in December, 1831, was as follows: "For nine years, gentlemen, I have used my best exertions in promoting the cause of internal improvements in the State. While collecting a great mass of local information, I have often reflected that Virginia did not avail herself immediately of advantages,

Several of these improvements are of especial interest to us. Applications were made to the Legislature in the early part of 1832 for a charter for a railway from Portsmouth, Virginia, to Weldon, North Carolina, and also for one for the Petersburg Railway. Both of these roads were built a few years later, and now run within a few miles of the scenes of the insurrection of 1831. They form, wth the Norfolk and Western, which was built in the latter part of this period, a triangle having its vertices at Norfolk, Petersburg, and Weldon. Within this triangle lies that part of Southampton county which was desolated by Nat Turner and his followers. The Chowan, Blackwater, Nottaway, and Meherrin rivers, which pass near these scenes, were improved for purposes of intercourse and commerce, and, together with the Three Creek, surround the same portion of Southampton, leaving one narrow passage at Belfield. The Legislature of 1831-32 also investigated the expediency of completing the Dismal Swamp Canal, which was considered of great economic advantage to Suffolk and the neighboring districts of Nansemond, Isle of Wight, Southampton and the other counties of the "Black Belt."

Nor had Virginia neglected her intellectual development. "The mass of education in Virginia before the Revolution," wrote Mr. Jefferson, "placed her with the

which, without a prophetic spirit, it may be said, will at some future day make the first State in the Union. To those less acquainted with her resources, and who have reflected less on her geographical situation and topographical features, this assertion may appear bold, but time will establish its correctness, when the circumstances which have hitherto embarrassed her progress shall have been modified; internal improvement itself is one of the means best calculated to effect this purpose." These circumstances were slavery and its necessary encumbrances, but the Legislature, which was in session at this time, took the suggestion of the Public Engineer and passed many bills for internal improvements and general economic progress.

foremost of her sister colonies."[1] These words are applicable also to the period of which we write. She had as complete a system of education as the majority of the States. Her university stood at the head of the arch and furnished a most liberal education to representative sons of every State in the Union. Her academies and private schools were excellent, and no educators in secondary schools were better known than Major Stone, of Brunswick; Frederick Coleman, of Concord Academy; Lewis Coleman, of Hanover Academy, and Rev. Peter Nelson, of "Wingfield," Hanover county. This debt was due chiefly to the inspiration and example of her illustrious statesmen, many of whom were still left to direct her energies. The convention called in 1829 to revise the State Constitution was so remarkable in its personnel as to evoke the statement that it was composed of more distinguished men than had ever assembled in any other public body in the United States. Among its members were Madison, Monroe, Marshall, John Randolph, and others who had occupied important positions under the State and Federal Governments.[2] Bishop Meade, the great Episcopal clergyman and historian, then in his prime, was one, and another was Commodore Matthew Fontaine Maury, who, by his charts of the winds and currents, had won from all the crowned heads of Europe and the scientific men of the world the title of "Geographer or Pathfinder of the Seas." Still another, John Mercer Brooke, by his "Deep Sea Sounding Apparatus," which had been suggested by the investigations of Maury, had enabled scientists to ascertain the character of the beds of the great plateau under the ocean between Newfoundland and Ireland. To Maury we are also indebted for the great network of submarine telegraphs, and the commerce of the world owes

[1] Randolph, Writings of Jefferson, vol IV, p. 23.
[2] Cooke, History of Virginia, p. 488.

him an incalculable obligation. The two most valuable general histories of Virginia appeared within the period under discussion—one by Robert R. Howison, in 1847, and the other by Charles Campbell, in 1849. The latter of these is especially valuable as a type of the best State histories. There were also many authors of fiction, and while Virginia literature of this period may not be of the first rank, yet it is valuable for its respect for good morals and manners and as an indication of her great impulse toward literary development. Nor should we forget the younger line of distinguished soldiers and statesmen, prominent among whom were John Y. Mason, the distinguished Cabinet officer and Minister to France, and Henry A. Wise, the statesman, soldier and author.

Notwithstanding these wise and patriotic citizens, to whose wisdom and sound judgment, no doubt, Virginia is indebted for the comparative quiet and prosperity which she enjoyed between 1830 and 1865, it would have been a wonderful phenomenon, had no signs of rebellion manifested themselves among the slaves, who had many facilities to learn the general progress of the times, the riots occurring, and the general party discussion in regard to their state of servitude. They, too, favored by the greater leniency of their owners, had advanced in intelligence, morals and manners. This was true, in spite of the unequal working of federal legislation and administration, which gave the majority of benefits to the non-slave holding, and most of the burdens to the slave-holding section. This was the point on which Southern discontent was aroused, and on which it rested until shifted to the dangers threatening slave property,[1] so that Madison might well prophetically exclaim, "The visible susceptibility to the contagion of nullification in the Southern States, the sympathy arising from known causes, and the

[1] Benton, Thirty Years in the United States Senate.

inculcated impressions of a permanent incompatibility of interest between the North and the South, may put it in the power of popular leaders, aspiring to the highest stations, to unite the South on some critical occasion in some course of action of which nullification may be the first step, secession the second, and a farewell separation, the last." It is indeed remarkable that there were only two attempts at insurrection during these thirty-five years— the one undertaken by a wild, fanatical negro at the beginning of the period, and the other led by a white fanatic, near its close. And this was the case, though every effort was made, at home and abroad, to cause discontent among the slaves and to incite them to impossible and murderous undertakings.[1]

Never in the history of slavery, however, was there less danger to owners, more contentment among the slaves themselves, fewer runaways, and greater advantages, social, financial, and political, gained from this institution. This was due partly to the fact that, though the country was filled with internal strife, the Union was gradually assuming the importance which had previously been held by the individual States. After the end of the war of 1812, which

[1] Thus, an Englishman, writing at the time, says that England's philanthropic zeal for the suppression of the slave trade covered their jealousy of the American commerce in Jamaica and in the Indian archipelago; that he regretted the hostile feeling growing up in England against America, all caused by the bitter harangues of American abolitionists, delegates from the American Anti-Slavery party; that Englishmen believed all these things coming from Americans, and truly longed for war on the boundary question, in order to hurl upon the slave States thousands of colored troops from Jamaica, and destroy the whole Union by a servile war.

William L. Garrison, the representative of the Anti-Slave Society, founded January 6, 1832, went to England in 1833, and was the means of the loss of all future influence of the American Colonization Society among the English Abolitionists.—Schouler's History of the United States, vol. IV., p. 215.

terminated our vital interest in European politics, that in domestic political questions became intense, and with these questions the introduction of direct foreign influence disappeared, very quickly followed by a reaction. to the extreme of intense dread of foreign influence. The people had learned to bear with the harangues of foreigners and to keep up with the course of foreign events, which had a marked influence on all classes of citizens, white and black, but direct foreign interference in governmental affairs was resented. The chief expression of this feeling was the "American," or "Know Nothing" party, which began about 1835, and, with varying power, manifested itself until the outbreak of the war between the States.[1] This, then, was a period of indirect foreign influence, when the pen was used instead of the sword, and foreigners worked through negro leaders and fanatics, instead of personal leadership. Consequently their personal influence could not be so strongly felt. Seeing that stealth was necessary, the slaves were no longer able to be deluded to such an extent by the hope of foreign aid, and grew to have more love for and faith in, the country which, apparently, they began to look upon as their native land. This was, however, not in all things the most fortunate period in Virginia history, for the reason that much of her best talent was directed against the attacks of the abolitionists, instead of being devoted to more profitable undertakings. The event which aroused that talent to the consideration of the slavery question more than any other, in that it involved grave danger to the slaves as well as to the State, was the Southampton insurrection of 1831.

[1] Ford, Federalist, p. 138.

CHAPTER II.

THE INSURRECTION.

DESCRIPTION OF SOUTHAMPTON COUNTY.—
Southampton county lies in the southeastern corner of
Virginia, in what is known, from its large negro population, as the "Black Belt," one hundred and fifty miles
south of the National Capital, Washington. It was a part
of "Warrasqueake," the Indian name for that region
known as Smith's Hundred, one of the original shires into
which Virginia was divided in 1634, extending from the
James River on the northeast to North Carolina on the
southwest. The name of this district was changed to Isle
of Wight Plantation in 1637, and, as by 1748 the population had become too numerous and its area too extensive
for one county, it was divided and that portion west of the
Blackwater River was called Southampton.[1]

This county can be taken as representative of eastern
Carolina and Virginia, its inhabitants being characterized
by the chivalrous spirit of the "Old North State," as well
as by the justly famed Virginia hospitality and family
pride. The relation between the two States is well
embodied in the words of Governor James Barbour, of Virginia, to Captain Calvin Jones, of Raleigh, North Carolina: "We turn with disgust and
horror from the foul blot in the characters of
men and dwell with peculiar complacency upon your generous friendship, so ennobling to our nature, enhanced by
the honorable mention you make of the aid furnished you
by our fathers in the hour of your distress, and the ac-

---

[1] In 1756 Governor Dinwiddie, in a list of tithables sent the
Lords of Trade, rates the population of Southampton at 973
whites and 1,036 blacks, a population greater than that of the Isle
of Wight in the same list.

knowledgment that the commingled blood of Virginia and North Carolina is the current of our connection." These words, written July 15, 1813, refer to the degrading deeds of the British troops in enticing away the slaves, inciting them to rebellion, and other acts of depredation, but they express the tie that has ever bound and will continue to bind together Virginia and North Carolina. The soil of the county is rich and the climate delightful, the two, with other circumstances, combining to make a noble, industrious, and liberty-loving population, well typifying the best Southern character. These people were alive to the progressive spirit of the age. Everywhere roads were being constructed and lands cleared. In the words of a most worthy citizen, who lived during this period: "Never were the people so progressive as between the year 1830 and the Civil War." Mr. James W. Parker said he was making money as rapidly as he cared to until the insurrection came along to interrupt him. For several years this delayed the progress of a portion of the county, and many citizens, becoming discouraged at the large destruction of property and life, sought other homes, but interest soon revived, and there was more effective energy and development than ever.[1]

Special attention was given to education. Schools and academies existed in great numbers. The Millfield Academy had been established in 1790 by a special act of the General Assembly, which empowered Benjamin Blunt and others to raise by lottery[2] money for this purpose. At the home of Mr. Thomas Pretlow there was an academy and another at Mr. James Parker's, both of

[1] The settlement of Indians in the county left their name in the "Indian words" on Nottoway River. Their lands were protected, and a special board of such citizens as James Trezevant, Benjamin Blunt, and William Urquhart, was appointed to look after their interests and education.

[2] This was the favorite means of raising money for internal improvements.

which were progressive, and at which were educated such public-spirited men as Capt. J. J. Darden and Gen. George H. Thomas. There were flourishing schools at Waller's and Mr. Nat Francis's. The Drewrysville Female Academy educated true Virginia women. The influence of the latter still lives in some of the model mothers and wives of the county. In this county were born and lived some of the most noted characters connected with the history of America, such as John Y. Mason, the statesman; George H. Thomas,[1] the soldier; William Mahone, the famous Virginia railroad president, Senator, and politician. Such were the citizens of 1831 and the years preceding 1865. The home of such progress, the mother of such men, and the scene of Nat Turner's massacre, Southampton is interesting as one of the historic counties of the United States.

DEVELOPMENT OF THE PLOT.—The month of August has been generally selected as the most suitable time of year for arousing the slaves to hostility; nor is this more remarkable than the fact that the quiet and stillness of some Saturday or Sunday night has been considered by the negroes most appropriate for the execution of schemes of murder and pillage. Only in a few instances has Christmas or some national holiday been selected for such purposes. This can be explained by the fact that Virginia was an agricultural State, there being comparatively few large farms at this time, and consequently much confidence and mutual intercourse between master and slave. By August the cultivation of the crops of corn, cotton, and tobacco was completed. There were only a few minor duties to be performed, which would be

1. In recognition of his gallantry in the Mexican War, General Thomas's native county presented him with a costly sword, which he prized above all gifts and deemed too precious to be worn except on the occasion of his marriage. This sword is now in the possession of General Thomas's sisters, Misses Judith and Fannie Thomas, of Newsom's Depot, Va.

allotted to the children, leaving the adults to hunt and fish and attend religious services. In fact, this month was the month of "jubilee," when it was a sacrilege to labor; it was the month of worship and camp-meetings, where week after week was spent, each person taking his tent and provisions with him, laying aside all temporal cares. It is impossible to describe the ease, happiness, and sense of security felt by all.

The servants had a freedom almost equal to their owners. Many of them were left at home to spend their holiday as they pleased, while those who delighted to attend the meetings of the whites had ample time to assemble and converse, and, after the services of the whites, to attend services conducted by ministers of their own color. But Saturday and Sunday were the principal leisure days. Saturday afternoon was a general holiday for all slaves who had been industrious and obedient during the week, when they could work their own crops and spend the time in fishing with their master's outfit or hunting with his gun.[1] By many, Sunday was spent in the same manner, but most of the slaves were very religious, and attended Sunday-school and church. No master could force a slave to work on the Sabbath. It was a pleasure to the master and his children to devote this day to worship with, and instruction of, the negroes. They generally worshiped together and had the same pastors. No church was built in the South without provisions for the negro servants.[2] And at the present day many will remember

[1] The broken and missing guns, etc., were the means by which many slaves were convicted in the massacre of 1831.

[2] Col. Robert Carter, known as "King Carter" from his ownership of so many slaves, rebuilt the historic Christ's Church, Lancaster county, in 1732, which was first built by his father John Carter in 1670, and he reserved a large portion of it for his slaves, besides a pew near the pulpit for his immediate family. Mead, Old Churches and Families, vol. II., pp. 116-118.

Gillie, in his "Historical Collections," vol. II., pp. 335-338, says of Rev. Samuel Davies: "From the year 1747, when Mr. Davies was settled in Virginia, to 1751, he baptized about forty

the invitation to commune given to the former slaves after the communion of the whites. Four days for Christmas, a week when the crops were "laid by," Easter, the

negroes, of whom he says he had as satisfying evidences of the sincere piety of several of them as he ever had from any person in his life. And in May, 1754, when he was at Edinburgh, concerning the affairs of New Jersey College, he said that when he left Virginia, in August, 1753, there was a hopeful appearance of a greater spread of religious concern among the negroes, and that a few weeks before he left home he had baptized in one day fifteen negroes, after they had been catechised for some months."

Mr. Fred Noble, in the "Redemption of Africa," says: "Negro Baptists to some extent are a monument of the religious activity of Southern white Baptists. In 1801 the Charleston Association petitioned the legislature of South Carolina to remove restrictions on the religious meetings of slaves.* * * Planters frequently paid liberally toward the support of home missionaries to the negroes. * * * Between 1845 and 1861 the white Southern Baptists did much for negro evangelization, but from 1865 till recently they showed only slight interest." The other churches were equally active in this line.

The Richmond Times of October 26, 1899, says: "The Northern people will never completely understand the relationship that existed between the Southern white man and his slave. The slaves were members of the family and were always treated as such from the old "mammy" down to the youngest child. When they were sick they had the attention of a physician, if necessary, and always the attention and nursing of the mistress of the household, who was herself a good doctor. Everything necessary to the comfort and welfare of the sick slave was done and with the same spirit that these noble women administered to the sick members of their immediate family. The bare suggestion that this was done from sordid motives is a shameful libel upon the best women that God ever made, for if there ever was a model woman in this world she was the Southern matron, who was always worshipped as the family saint and who fairly lived up to the responsibilities of that exalted position.

"Another thing in this connection. The women of the South, old and young, matrons and maids, whom the North had pictured as 'indolent, exclusive and indifferent to the sorrow and distress and ignorance of the slaves,' spent a goodly portion of their time in training the minds and morals of the black members of their household. On the large plantations there was a chapel, where services were held every Sunday, when and where the slaves were gathered to receive religious instruction. In the smaller family circles the slaves were assembled on the Sabbath in some convenient place and 'ole Mis' and young Mis' ' read the Bible to them and taught them the way of life."

No doubt these facts partly account for the superiority of the American missionary of today in Africa.

Fourth of July, and other holidays through the year were allowed the slaves. In addition, they seem to have been allowed the free disposal of the entire night, which might be spent in sleep, attending dances, corn and cotton matches, or in hunting for the "'possum and the coon."[1] On all of these occasions the negroes were trusted, and no one could be persuaded that his slaves would be guilty of a breach of this confidence.

Such a Saturday and Sunday were the 20th and 21st of August, 1831. Many of the ringleaders of the plot that was forming had been especially industrious and obedient, and consequently had been permitted to have holiday on Saturday. To escape all suspicion, the ringleader feigned sickness and refused to go to the dining room as usual for his meals. He was afraid that the kindness of his mistress would soften his heart and cause him to show his guilt. But with her own hands she prepared him a special supper and took it to him. Sunday was even more quiet, if possible, and unruffled by suspicion. Mr. Joseph Travis, the master of the two leaders of this band, with his family, attended services at church in the morning, and, as was the custom of this neighborhood, went home with friends, not returning to his plantation until late Sunday evening. But the slaves had not been idle. They had been going from house to house collecting for a feast which was to be held that day. Hark, the second in command of the gang, had gone several miles away to procure cider and provisions. On Saturday three slaves—Henry Edwards, Hark Travis, and Nat Turner—had agreed to prepare a dinner for the men they expected the next day, and there to concert plans of action, as they had not previously agreed upon one. So, on the following day, Hark brought a pig and Henry brandy, and, being

---

[1] It was a negro who had been hunting that first discovered and reported the hiding place of Nat Turner.

joined by other slaves—Sam, Nelson, Will, and Jack, they prepared the proposed feast on the banks of the Cabin Ford, near Travis's.[1] There it was decided that they should begin that night at their master's and murder all the white people of the county, sparing neither age nor sex. It was a beautiful Sabbath and not the least suspicion had been aroused of their intention. Such was the quiet and peace of mind of the inhabitants on this beautiful Sabbath that many of them had gone to Gates county, North Carolina, to attend a camp-meeting, and those who remained at home deemed it useless to lock the doors of their houses, which were left open to receive the fresh breeze of this balmy August night. They felt safer for the reason that the slaves were there to keep guard. But a few were destined to betray this trust.

The instigator of this plot was Nat Turner, a wild, fanatical Baptist preacher, born the property of Mr. Benjamin Turner, on October 2, 1800, just five days before the execution of Gabriel Prosser, who, in August of that year, incited the slaves of Richmond and vicinity to rebellion. The notorious John Brown had been born just five months before Nat. Thus 1800 was an important year in the history of slave insurrections in Virginia, the date of the birth of the leaders of the two last and most important insurrections in the South, and of the Gabriel Insurrection of Henrico county and vicinity. It is an interesting coincidence that Gabriel was executed on the 7th of October, Nat Turner captured on the 31st, and John Brown on the 17th of the same month.

After the death of his master, Nat became the property of Mr. Samuel Turner, brother of Ben Turner, whose widow the insurgents later murdered. Mr. Thomas Moore

[1]This place now belongs to Mr. Joshua Powell, of Boykin's district.

Site of Residence of Mr. Joseph Travis.

afterward bought him, and at his death left him to his son Putnam. Mrs. Moore had married Mr. Joseph Travis,[1] and this explains why Nat had been living with the latter since 1830, and why he was often called Nat Travis. He had always been fortunate in having a kind and indulgent owner. He acknowledged this, and seemed to love his mistress and her children. Though he had never been sold out of Boykins District, yet he was thoroughly acquainted with every by-path and corner in the county, and had gained many social and intellectual advantages. He had at the time of the massacre developed into a stout, black negro of the pure African type, but in childhood he had been delicate and consequently was more indulged than was usual. Exceedingly precocious in his youth, he developed into a man of considerable mental ability and wide information, especially in the sciences. He learned much in the Sunday-schools, where the text books for the small children were the ordinary speller and reader, and that for the older negroes the Bible. Nat said that he learned to read with so much ease that he did not know when he learned it, and when a book was given him one day to stop his crying he began spelling the names of the different objects. This story made a great impression, not only on his mind, but on the minds of the neighbors. But it is well known that Mr. J. C. Turner, his young master, gave him instruction, assisted by Nat's parents, who seem to have been intelligent negroes. His mother, Nancy, is said to have been imported directly from Africa, and to have been so wild that at Nat's birth she had to be tied to prevent her from murdering him. She later developed into a useful and faithful servant. His father was also

[1] It is very probable that this man was related to the Travis family of Jamestown, and, if so, was from one of the distinguished families of Virginia. Champion Travis is an historical character in the history of Virginia of the Revolutionary Period.

very high-spirited, and ran away when Nat was a boy, and was never recaptured.

Nat himself had, up to the time of the insurrection, been faithful and highly trusted, and was made an overseer. In fact, he was quite unrestricted, and, being a preacher, was allowed many privileges. There was only one person who mistrusted him, and that was Mr. Salathiel Francis, the brother of Mrs. Travis, who told her that Nat was a negro of bad character, and that it would be best for her not to trust him so much. But, thinking her brother somewhat uncompromising, wild and reckless in general, she continued lenient with Nat. Nat's son, Redic, survived him and proved to be a worthy and highly respected slave, much like his father in ability, but not fanatical. There are still many of his relatives living in Southampton, and one of them, though now in the lunatic asylum at Petersburg, Virginia, well illustrates the trend of his early ancestors. Intelligent and well informed on most subjects, this man, Hack Brown, is at times wild and raving, bearing a special grudge against the officers of the institution, as may be natural with lunatics, but he also seems to be a religious fanatic, and in response to any question will reply, "So saith the Lord."[1]

From childhood Nat was very religious, truthful, and honest, "never owning a dollar, never uttering an oath, never drinking intoxicating liquors, and never committing a theft." He never had any cause to steal, as he always had plenty, but he often did the planning for negroes on plundering expeditions, as they trusted his superior generalship and ability.

Nat's own words, better than those of any other, will give an insight into the development of his character, illustrate his treatment as a slave, and show how his mind, attempting to grapple with things beyond its reach,

[1] Dr. William F. Drewry, Superintendent of Asylum.

Nat Turner.

observant of everything that was passing, it is easy to suppose that religion would be the subject to which it would be directed; and, although this subject principally occupied my thoughts, there was nothing that I saw, or heard of it to which my attention was not directed."

Count Marboeuf predicted that Napoleon would create for himself a path of more than ordinary splendor.[1] So others had impressed upon him the greatness in store for him, until he believed Providence had destined him for the master of the world. A person may hear or tell a story over and over again, until it is so vividly impressed upon his mind that he finally believes that it happened, as was the case with the little boy who related that he was sitting on the doorsteps when his parents were married. Thus Nat believed that these things had actually been told him by the Lord, and his earnestness and intellectual superiority impressed all the negroes who saw him with the truth of his claims. Their astonishment did not escape his notice and made him believe all the more that he was to be a great man and the deliverer of his race.

Thus surrounded by religious and educated persons, in whom he had the utmost confidence, and having parents and grandparents who had been instructed by their owners, this restless, inquisitive, and observant youth, daily impressed with the consciousness of his superior intellect and religion, was incited to a life of seclusion from his fellow-servants, praying, experimenting in casting different things in molds made of earth, and trying to make paper, gunpowder and many other articles.[2] His master was a coach-maker, and in his labors with this workman Nat had become quite expert in mending such articles as tin buckets, old bells, etc., and in making into various

---

[1] Abbott, History of Napoleon, vol. I, p. 22.

[2] Upon examination, it was found that he had much knowledge of these subjects and was well acquainted with the movements of the planets, etc.

useful forms the old iron and wood taken to him by his fellow-servants. Taking them to the woods, he would skillfully transform them as desired, and returning them to their owners nicely polished in the shape of a sword or any desired article, he would impress these credulous beings with a sense of his superiority.

Recognizing the fact that to be great he must appear so, he wrapped himself in mystery and allowed his mind to be occupied with religious notions. He faithfully attended religious meetings, and, being very ambitious, he was struck with the text, "Seek ye the Kingdom of God; and all these things shall be added unto you." As he was one day praying at his plow the spirit repeated the text, which greatly astonished him. By the spirit, he said, he meant the spirit that spoke to the prophets of old. Praying continually for two years, whenever his duties would permit, he again had the same revelation, which fully convinced him that he was ordained for some great purpose in the hands of the Almighty. Several years having rolled around, in which many events occurred to strengthen him in this belief, his mind forcibly reverted to the admiring remarks made of him in his childhood, and the supernatural things that he believed had been shown him. So, having arrived at manhood, seeing himself still a slave, and knowing the influence he had obtained over the minds of his fellow-servants, by his austerity and air of mysticism, he determined to prepare the negroes for an uprising by telling them that something was about to happen which would fulfill a great promise which had been made to him. But about this time he was put under an overseer whom he did not like, no doubt because he had been accustomed to more privileges, so he ran away. After 30 days, however, he returned, to the astonishment of some of the negroes, who murmured against him and said, if they had Nat's sense, they would not serve any master in the world. The reason he returned was that he imagined the spirit appeared to him and told him that he had his wishes directed towards the things of this world and not to the Kingdom of Heaven, and that he should return to the service of his earthly master, "for," said the spirit, "he who knoweth his master's will and doeth it not shall be beaten with many stripes, and thus have I chastened you." He also saw a vision which revealed white spirits and black spirits contending in battle, the sun darkened, the thunders rolling in the heavens and blood flowing in streams, and a voice spoke unto him, saying: "Such is your luck, such are you called to see, and let it come rough or smooth, you must surely bear it."

He now withdrew himself as much as possible from the intercourse of his fellow-servants in order to serve more freely the spirit, which had again appeared to him and reminded him of the things which it had already shown him, and promised that it would then reveal to him the knowledge of the elements, the revolutions of the planets, the operation of the tides and the changes of the seasons. This was in 1825, and he began to believe that he had been made perfect in faith and holiness and that the Holy Spirit was saying to him: "Behold me in the heavens." He said he looked and saw the forms of men in different attitudes, and lights in the sky, which he called the hands of the Savior, stretched forth from east to west. Wondering greatly at these miracles, he prayed to be informed of their meaning, and shortly afterwards, while laboring in the field, he discovered drops of blood on the corn, as though it were dew from heaven. He communicated this fact to many, both white and black. He found on the leaves in the forest hieroglyphic characters and numbers, with the forms of men in different attitudes, portrayed in blood and representing the figures he had seen in the heavens. He took some of these to his mistress and told her that they were signs shown him by the Lord, but she

Nat Turner's Bible.

only dismissed him with her usual kind and indulgent words. Nat, however, perceived in them the explanations of the signs which he had seen in the heavens, and believed, he said, that the Savior was about to lay off the yoke which he had borne for the sins of men, and that the great day of judgment was at hand. He told these things to a white man—Ethelred T. Brantley[1]—on whom it had a wonderful effect, and who, in Nat's words, "ceased from his wickedness and was attacked immediately with a cutaneous eruption, and blood oozed from the pores of his skin, and after praying and fasting nine days he was healed." Believing themselves converted, and that the Savior commanded them to be baptized, he and Nat proceeded to Persons' mill pond and in turn baptized each other in the sight of many who had been attracted hither by curiosity.

Nat said: "On the 12th of May, 1828, I heard a loud voice in the heavens and the spirit instantly appeared to me and said the serpent was loosed and Christ had laid down the yoke he had borne for the sins of men, and that I should take it on and fight against the serpent, for the time was fast coming when the first should be last and the last should be first." He now felt certain of his work, and only waited for the sign in heaven to tell him to begin, until which time he was to make his plan known to no one, but, on the appearance of the sign, he was to arise and slay his enemies with their own weapons. This sign he recognized in the eclipse of the sun, in February, 1831, and, immediately conceiving the seal to be removed from his lips, he communicated the work to be done to his four confidants—Henry Porter, Hark Travis, Nelson Williams,[2] and Sam Francis. They planned to begin

[1] This man was a respectable overseer, but after his intercourse with Nat no one would have anything to do with him, so, it is said, he left the State.

[2] This Nelson was the brother of the wife of Jeff. Edwards, who distinguished himself in his efforts to save his master's family and other white people.

their work of death on the 4th of July, but Nat's mind was so impressed with the greatness of the plot and the various schemes for its accomplishment that he fell sick and the time passed. It was not to take place on the day of Independence, and it is possible that Nat only saw the danger of keeping this date after its selection. For special arrangements had been made for celebrating it, and men, having assembled at every public place, would have more readily suppressed this undertaking then than was possible a few days later. But the time was not spent in idleness. The negroes continued to form and reject new plans, until Nat imagined that his sign had again appeared unto him. The sign now was the peculiar appearance of the sun on the morning of August 13th. The sun's disk seemed, on rising, to have changed from its usual brilliant golden color to a pale, greenish tint, which soon gave place to cerulean blue, and this also to a silvery white, all owing to some change or derangement of the atmosphere of the sun. In the afternoon it appeared as an immense circular plane of polished silver, and to the naked eye there was exhibited upon its surface an appearance that was termed a "black spot." The sun shone with a dull, gloomy light, and the atmosphere was moist and hazy. These phenomena excited much astonishment and wonder among the people generally. The superstitious believed that some awful calamity was about to happen, while the speculations of the more intelligent citizens appeared unsatisfactory.[1] The conspirators took advantage of the excitement and fixed upon the night of Sunday, August 21, 1831, as the date upon which to put their plot into execution.

The feast of the conspirators began in the morning on Sunday, but Nat, as was his custom, again exhibited

[1] Forest, Historical and Descriptive Sketches of Norfolk: Howison, History of Virginia. In "Judith" Marion Harland describes the excitement that existed among the whites and colored.

Persons' Mill Pond.

shrewdness in not joining them until about 3 o'clock in the afternoon, thus giving his men time for eating and drinking, while he retained his usual reserve and consequence, which he knew were the only means by which he could succeed. On going up, Nat saluted them, and seeing Will,[1] whom he had not informed of the scheme, in the company, with great caution and foresight he asked him how came he there. This fellow showed by his answer that he was a most cruel and determined convert to the cause, as, with his broadax, he amply afterwards proved to be. He replied that his life was worth no more than others', and his liberty as dear to him, and that he would obtain this or lose his life. This satisfied the "general," and as Jack[2] was a mere tool in the hands of Hark, they soon had their plans arranged. Now were to begin those frightful scenes of the memorable year 1831, in Boykin's District, near Cross Keys.

THE RAID.—The section of the county embraced in the raid was the most recently settled, and the inhabitants had not reached that stage of larger cultivated estates and imposing dwellings enjoyed by the farmers of the more eastern counties. The country was thinly settled, consequently the blacks, concealed by the large expanse of forest which surrounded them, could quietly enjoy their reveling undetected. In this lonely den they remained until ten o'clock in the night. Ample time having been given the hardy farmers and their families to become composed in sleep, these fanatics, in the solemn stillness of the night, proceeded to murder the best friends

---

[1] He belonged to Mr. Nathaniel Francis.

[2] Jack was indeed weak, as the records of the county show, and Hark, who married his sister, being an influential negro, wouldn't let him go home when he pleaded sick. Colonel Worth, who saw Hark after his capture, said he was one of the most perfectly framed men he ever saw—a regular black Apollo.

they had on earth—Mr. Joseph Travis and his family.[1]
On reaching the yard, they met another negro—Austin—
who made the eighth member of their band. All except
Nat went to the cider press and drank their fill, thus
beginning a course which would the sooner, and ultimately did, lead to their ruin. They seemed to hesitate
before making a start, but the die was cast, and, proceeding to the house, they consulted as to the best manner
of entering. Hark, Nat's lieutenant, proposed to break
open the door with his axe. He knew that the excited
victims would be no match for them. Nat's cool and wise
judgment, however, prevailed. Hark placed against the
chimney a ladder upon which Nat ascended to the upper-
most window. Quietly he descended the stairs, removed
the guns from their places, and then opened the doors to
his comrades.

Nat said he could not kill his kind master and mistress,
and the task was made doubly hard when the little baby,
which he had often fondled, looked him in the face and
sweetly smiled, as he reached down to take it in his arms.
This was more than even he could stand, and he put it
back in the cradle, to remain in safety until the negroes
had got some distance from the house. Then, remem-
bering his resolve to spare neither age nor sex, and reflect-
ing, as he said, that "nits make lice," Nat sent Henry and
Will back to take it by its heels and dash its brains out
against the bricks of the fireplace. But the followers
decided that the leader was to strike the first blow. One
hatchet and a broad-ax seem to have been their only
weapons. This was a small beginning for a massacre
which was not quelled until the perpetrators numbered

[1] The Cabin Pond was on Mr. Giles Reese's farm and nearer
to his home than to Travis's. Mr. Reese asked Nat on the gallows
why he slighted him, and Nat replied: "Marse Giles, you were
too powerful a man to begin with, and besides we were afraid
of your two fierce bulldogs. But we were going to return to you
after we had collected a sufficient force."

at least sixty, all mounted and armed with every conceivable weapon.

Miss Maria Pope, who lived at Travis's, and for whom Nat had a special dislike, had been chosen as the first victim, but she was away on a visit and thus escaped. So Nat and Will entered their master's chamber. The darkness and, no doubt, a remorseful conscience were the means of saving Nat from the guilt of the murder of his own friends and protectors. Nat's hatchet glanced and Mr. Travis sprang from his bed, calling for his wife. These were his last words. Will struck him dead with his axe. Mrs. Travis was at least fortunate in one respect—she was spared the horror of witnessing the terrible death of her husband. One blow was sufficient to dispatch her. Putnam Moore, Nat's young master, and Joel Westbrook,[1] who was apprenticed to Mr. Travis, lads of sixteen, were sleeping in an upper chamber. Both were murdered in their sleep. These people had been murdered quietly in order to avoid any possible alarm. Quite a different course was pursued after the number of the band was increased. They took here four guns and several muskets, a pound or two of powder and shot, besides several horses and other instruments suitable for their bloody work. To impose a sort of discipline upon them, Nat formed his band in line as soldiers, took them through all the manoeuvres with which he was acquainted, and paraded them up and down for some time in the barn-yard. In the meantime they had decorated themselves in the most ludicrous and fantastic style, with feathers in their hats and long red sashes around their waists and over their shoulders.[2]

[1] He now rests in the family burying-ground, owned by his brother, Mr. James D. Westbrook, of Drewrysville, Virginia.

[2] The sashes were made of the blood-red material with which the tops of the old-fashioned gigs were lined, and when this gave out, they used sheets dyed in the blood of their victims. The "old-fashioned" gig somewhat resembled the modern "dog-cart." It had two wheels, and, being very tall, was overturned at the least provocation.

A quarter of a mile to the southeast dwelt Mr. Salathiel Francis, a brother of Mrs. Travis. This gentleman was a bachelor, living in a small, single-room house, with no one but a faithful slave—Nelson. He was a powerful man, brave, determined, and unmindful of death. No one knew this better than these eight negroes, and they were certain that he would make quick work of them if they broke his door open. After proceeding, then, silently and in good order to this place, they concluded to secure him in an artful manner. Sam and Will were slaves of Mr. Nat Francis. They called to Mr. Salathiel Francis and told him that they had a note from his brother. Unarmed and unsuspicious, he went to the door in his night clothes. When he opened it they seized him and by repeated blows over the head murdered him while bravely defending himself and calling to Nelson for his gun. But Nelson had to see to his own life. He was known to be loyal. They shot him, but he managed to escape through the back door,[1] and was instrumental in saving the life of the wife of his master's brother.

Continuing to bear to the southeast for half a mile, the negroes reached the home of a Mrs. Harris. She was a widow with several children and grandchildren. The insurgents passed through the yard of this farmhouse, but no one was killed, nor was any depredation committed. Unfortunately no one asked Nat why this was, but the slaves said that one of their number—Joe Harris —refused to join the band unless they promised to spare

---

[1] To see this house of one story and a "jump" might dispel a prevalent idea in the Northern section of the country that the life of the Virginian has been one of selfish luxury and ease. Many owning a smaller number of slaves, while constricted in provision for their own families, yet maintained, in every humane provision, the well being of their servitors and dependents, and in doing this constantly disregarded their own comfort. This is true of the treatment of old family negroes at the present day.

Home of Mr. Salathiel Francis.

THE SOUTHAMPTON INSURRECTION.   39

his "white people." Whether this is true or whether it was offered as a means of rescuing Joe from the gallows cannot be ascertained. However, circumstances are in favor of the version. Being appreciative, though ignorant, this frightened negro did not see the necessity of killing all the whites, especially a family of women and children, and, besides, when threatened with the loss of his life, he probably deemed it best to accept the proposition in order to see if their professions of ultimate success would prove true. In either case, he may have intended the welfare of his people. He possibly intended to escape, but after seeing the success at the next plantation, decided it was useless to do so. The leaders, as they had not made one addition to their number, very likely were glad, under any condition, even at the expense of their maxim "to kill all," to make recruits.[1] He was hanged, however, as after the suppression of the band he had returned home dressed in the clothes of Mr. Peebles, who had been killed at the Turner farm. So quietly and cautiously had the insurgents formed their plan that the next morning the family were unconscious of their narrow escape, and proceeded to their daily tasks. The children went to school, several miles away, and it was an hour or more before they were warned of the state of affairs. They had met a negro, George Porter, who advised them to go home, as the British were killing all the people in the country. But, being small, and giving but little credence to this report, they proceeded to school, within a few miles of which the insurgents were at that time. This negro George was believed by the grown people, however, who had by this time heard the same report from other sources. The cruel-

[1] Mrs. James Barnes (nee Miss Bettie Powell), granddaughter of Mrs. Harris, and then a child of eight years of age, living at this place.

ties of the British at Hampton in 1812 were still remembered and also lent credence to the report.[1]

The Newsom place, a short distance from Mrs. Harris', was left to the right, and, continuing their southeastern course for a mile, the negroes came to Mrs. P. Reese's.[2] The door of the house was unlocked. Mrs. Reese and her son William were asleep within. The former was killed without being aroused from her slumbers. The latter, who was in another room, called to know who was there, but he was not long kept in doubt. Mr. James Barmer was manager of this farm and was in the house. He awoke and tried to escape, but was discovered and rendered helpless by repeated blows from axes and grubbing hoes. At first he called for help, but soon decided that it was better to feign death. Wounded and bleeding and kicked about, he bore it patiently and survived. Several days later he was found in this exhausted condition, his wounds exposed and festered. It left him maimed for life and ever afterwards unable to do manual labor.

The next place visited by Nat and his associates was the house of Mr. Wiley Francis,[3] who lived three miles to the south of the Reese farm. Mr. Francis, notwithstanding the pleading of his wife and daughters, refused to flee. They were hid in the woods and provisioned by faithful slaves, who had declared that they would die for the whites, and took their stations in the yard to await the arrival of the insurgents. These soon put in their appearance and were greeted by Mr. Francis with "Here I am, boys; I will not go from my home to be killed!" His

[1] So accurate was George's description of the route taken by the insurgents and of the victims killed that people believed afterwards that he had joined the gang, but his heart failing him he had returned, as did several others. He was not harmed, however, but lived an obedient servant, dying several years after the War of Secession.

[2] This farm is now owned by Mr. William Powell.

[3] Mr. Henry Smith now owns this farm.

THE SOUTHAMPTON INSURRECTION. 41

slaves then warned Nat's band that they could not come farther than the fence without losing their lives. They pleaded that they were thirsty and asked for water and also brandy, but the faithful negroes saw through this pretense. Perceiving that it was useless to resist further, Nat remarked that the old man was not worth killing, but that he would be taken later and his slaves forced to yield. These threats neither affected the slaves, who were wise enough to see the folly of such a reckless attempt, nor the master, who sat peacefully in his door and declared he would suffer death before he would run. So the attempt was abandoned.[1]

Several miles to the northeast of Mr. Francis' and one mile east of the home of Mrs. Reese was the residence of a widow, Mrs. Elizabeth Turner. It was now sunrise on Monday morning. A rush was made for the distillery, which was located on the side of the lane which led to the house. Mr. Hartwell Peebles, the overseer, was there. He was immediately shot down by Austin and his clothes appropriated by one of the band. There were some, however, who were not only bent on plunder, but who wished to gratify their bloody passions. They advanced to the dwelling. With repeated blows from the axe which had hitherto wrought such execution in the hands of Will, the door,[2] which had been locked at their approach, was broken open, and Will, seizing Mrs. Turner, dispatched her, while Nat, taking Mrs. Newsom by the hand, struck

[1] Nat did not mention this visit in his confession, but it seems very probable. It is based on the evidence of those who heard Mrs. Lavinia Francis relate it. Nat may have left this out, as he did other facts, which showed the spirit of the majority of the slaves, the cowardice of his men and the discouragement he met with on all sides. Besides his followers were still few in number and thus offered less inducement to join than advantage in resisting them, to slaves accustomed to the orders of their kind master.

[2] The gashes are still to be seen on the door and the blood on the floor of his house, which is owned by Mr. Elias Vick.

her several blows over the head. His sword was too dull, so this murder was committed also by the murderer of Mrs. Turner. Trembling, frightened nearly to death, and pleading for their lives, these defenseless women were pitilessly slaughtered. The next business in order was the destruction of property and a search for money and ammunition.

Although several plantations had now been visited, on all of which there were a number of slaves, the company consisted of only fifteen men, six on foot and nine mounted. They now decided to divide, as they did also on several occasions afterwards, roaming the country in squads, but always uniting at some fixed point. Those on foot proceeded through a by-path to the home of Mr. Henry Bryant, several hundred yards to the northeast. After Mr. Bryant, his wife and child, and his wife's mother had been killed, and the programme of plunder and destruction repeated, the blacks turned towards Mrs. Catherine Whitehead's,[1] whither their companions had gone. This place was one mile east of Mrs. Turner's, but they found the work had been completed there and the gang ready to march when they arrived.

Mrs. Whitehead was a wealthy lady, known throughout Eastern Virginia and North Carolina for her hospitality.[2] Mr. Richard Whitehead,[3] one of the sons, a Methodist preacher, was in the cotton patch with his slaves when the negroes rode up the lane to the house. He asked one of his servants what all that meant, but his slave seemed not to know. Mr. Whitehead, though addressed as "Dick" by the gang and ordered to come to them, without hesitation obeyed and was attacked and cut to pieces

[1] This place belongs to Mr. John Sykes. The Bryant place is owned by Mr. Vick.

[2] The Whiteheads of Virginia are members of this family. Many of them are famous preachers and lawyers.

[3] He had just returned from feeding his hogs.

The Turner Farm.

by Will's fatal axe.[1] This occurred near an old cedar tree, which still stands to mark the spot. Even when attacked, he was ignorant of the meaning of it all, and the more he asked why they were killing him, the louder the band yelled, "Kill him! Kill him!" They were determined that none should escape. Nat pursued a servant girl who fled at their approach, but, perceiving her to be colored, he returned to the scene of the murder. His companions had not been idle. Three daughters, and a child, who was receiving its morning bath at the hands of a loving grandmother, had been murdered. Will was dragging the mother of the family from the house as Nat approached. She told him that she did not wish to live since all of her children had been murdered, so, in Nat's presence, Will severed her head from her body. But there were two daughters still alive. Miss Margaret concealed herself in the space formed by the projection of the cellar cap from the house between two brick chimneys, but she fled and was pursued by Nat and killed with a fence rail, repeated blows with his sword being insufficient for the purpose. This is the only murder that Nat directly committed.

Hubbard was a servant of this family. He and a majority of the slaves of his mistress remained faithful and were valuable witnesses at the trials of Nat's gang. When they approached, Hubbard hid his young mistress, Miss Harriet, between the bed and the mat. After the murderers left he went for her and said: "Miss Harriet, thank God, you are saved. Don't stay here; come along with me to the

---

[1]The day before he had preached at Barnes' Church, which is about thirty miles to the southeast, near the Carolina line; and at this protracted meeting the concluding hymn was,

"How happy every child of grace
Who feels his sins forgiven."

A worthy prelude to so untimely a death.

woods." She obeyed and remained there while this loyal man returned to the house and procured food and bedding. But she began to fear that he had returned for the insurgents, so she changed her hiding place. True to his faith, the old man returned and she heard him in his grief moan out, "Oh, Lord, they have caught her!" Still frightened, the poor girl refused to show herself, and allowed the disconsolate protector to return to the house. The next day some soldiers on the trail of the blacks arrived, and, having heard Hubbard's story, told him to go again to search for his mistress. Terribly bitten by the mosquitoes, she had suffered enough to heed any succor. She disclosed herself, but was afraid to go to the house, so she wrote on a shingle signs which convinced the whites that she was alive. She was rescued and taken to Cross Keys.[1] In a single grave in one corner of the garden, not one hundred yards from the door of this historic home, rest the bodies of her seven relatives, a monument to base cruelty and barbarity, as that of Miss Harriet, near by, is one to witness the devotion of a faithful slave and to show that slavery in Virginia was not such as to arouse rebellion, but was an institution which nourished the strongest affection and piety in slave and owner, as well as moral qualities worthy of any age of civilization.

One party now traveled about a mile to the west to Mr. Trajan Doyle's, and thence a few hundred yards towards Mr. Howell Harris'; the second party took a northward course to Mr. Richard Porter's and Mr. Nathaniel Francis', who lived, respectively, about one and two miles away. Mr. Doyle was found on his way to the mill,

[1] But what was this lone individual to do? All of her people had been murdered, and the old homestead was haunted by the cries and prayers of her dear ones. She adapted herself bravely to circumstances, however, and spent the remainder of her days in this home, surrounded by the slaves who had proved loyal and true, notwithstanding the persuasions and threats of members of their own race.

Home of Mrs. Catherine Whitehead.

accompanied by his servant, Hugh. The former was ruthlessly murdered, but the latter, instead of joining the insurgents, made his way home to save his mistress and her baby. Rushing into the house, he seized and dragged them to the thicket of an old graveyard, not taking time to tell his story until they were safely concealed. In this way he robbed the negroes of two of their intended victims.

This band was joined by other negroes, who informed them that Mr. Harris[1] had made his escape, having been warned of the insurrection by a mulatto girl, Mary. Consequently they were retracing their course, when they met Nat, who learned at Mr. Porter's that the alarm had spread. The blacks had been spreading destruction far and wide for eight or nine hours and not the least alarm had been given until now. The second squad had been at Mr. Porter's, but the mulatto girl had given them the alarm also and they had made their escape to the woods. They then advanced to the home of Mr. Nathaniel Francis. Hark or Will must have been in command of this division. When they arrived Mr. Francis was away. That morning a little negro boy, simple and stammering, had rushed over from Mr. Francis' sister's, Mrs. Travis, and related that some "folks had killed all the white folks" at his master's. Mr. Francis smiled and said: "You don't know what you are talking about." But whether this indifference was to evade all appearance of alarm or from incredulity, he was impressed sufficiently to ride over to investigate. His mother also went through a by-path to see if she could be of any assistance. It was in this manner that these lives were saved. The negroes had indeed been there and had gone away by a southeastern direction as Mr. Francis appeared from the northeast. He

[1]Mr. Howell Harris married the daughter of Mr. Wiley Francis. His farm and the Doyle farm (sometimes called the J. C. Turner place) belong to Mr. Hines.

was returning home, when he met some men, who told him his own people had been killed and that he must join them to form a guard. So, deeming it useless to return, he took his mother to a farmhouse on Pate's Hill, in the rear of the operations of the gang. She remained there until later in the day, while he set out to join the guard.

It appears that these men, having gone to the home of Mr. Francis, had found no one alive. But one person had been saved. In those days a young farmer always built his house so that it might be enlarged as his means increased. The usual style of house for a farmer of small means consisted of one square room on the first floor, with what was called a "jump" above and a kitchen in the rear. This was the style of the Francis house. The "jump" was fashioned into a neat and serviceable room by lathing and plastering it in such a manner as to form a semi-cylindrical apartment with a window in each gable end. Thus there were considerable spaces between the roof and the plastering, which were called cuddies, and used for "plunder" rooms and were accessible by doors near the end. These recesses were very dark. It was in one of these that Mrs. Lavinia Francis, the wife of this energetic farmer, was concealed by old "Red"[1] Nelson, who had been forced to flee from the murderers of his master.

[1] He was called "Red" Nelson to distinguish him from another negro of the same name, who was black. "Red" Nelson was a mulatto. He had been sold to a slave dealer and was to be sent South, but at his own solicitation he had been bought and kept in Virginia. He amply repaid this service, and no one recognized this more than his neighbors. After this he was the real master of the plantation, receiving and entertaining the gentlemen who visited his master. A gentleman who knew him well relates that he has seen him drink with the whites, and that he went wherever he pleased, from one section of the county to another, hospitality received at every home, where his deeds were fully esteemed and commended. He lived at Mr. Nat Francis' until after the Civil War, and then he went to Ohio.

Barnes' M. E. Church.

When the blacks asked for her, Nelson pretended to sympathize with them and joined heartily in the search. He went to the cuddy and shoved aside baskets, clothes, etc., but took special pains not to betray his mistress. She was also favored by the dark clothes in which she was dressed. Then, turning away, Nelson said she must be in the garden concealed behind the tall cabbage. As the negroes came out of the house they met Mrs. John K. Williams and her little child in the lane. This lady was the wife of Mr. "Choctaw" Williams,[1] and as he was teaching school she had decided to spend the day with Mrs. Francis. With her infant she was murdered before she reached the house. Mrs. Williams being taken for Mrs. Francis, no further search was made for the latter.

Two little boys named Brown, nephews of Mr. Francis, lived with him. He was their guardian, since both of their parents were dead. The younger of them, about three years of age, was standing in the lane as the negroes rode up, and ran to meet them, begging that he might ride, as he had probably often done of the plowmen as they returned from their work. He was taken up, to be cast down with his head severed from his body. At this sight his eight-year-old brother, who was hid near by in the weeds of the barn-yard, screamed out. He was caught, and suffered the fate of his brother. The negroes were then on their way to the "still," which was generally the rendezvous. Mr. Henry Doyle, the overseer and "stiller," saw them coming and ran to the house to tell Mrs. Francis of the danger. He was shot down as he emerged from the front door just under the cuddy in which this lady was hid. She had heard the screams of her nephews and had now to listen to the groans of Mr. Doyle. She could stand it no longer, and fainted. It is well she did, other-

---

[1] He was so called because he wore his hair in waves down his back and resembled an Indian in some respects.

wise she might have revealed her place of concealment, as her nephew had done. When she revived the negroes had drunk their fill of cider-wine, and many of them, much intoxicated, had proceeded on their journey, having been joined by nearly all of the family slaves. Much frightened, Mrs. Francis emerged from her cuddy and descended the stairs. She had heard some of her servants quarreling, and as she reached the door she saw them dividing her wedding dresses. They were very much surprised to see her, and one of them said: "I thought you were dead," and, making for her with a dirk, continued, "If you are not dead you shall soon be." But the other negro, Easter, who had belonged to her before her marriage to Mr. Francis, rushed up and said: "You shall not kill my mistress, who has been so kind to me. Touch her if you dare and I will kill you." Mrs. Francis then asked where the negroes were, and the wicked Charlotte replied that they had gone, but would be back to dinner, as they had killed several chickens for the purpose. Without further delay, except to hang up her keys and to take from the rack a home-made cheese, she went in search of her husband with Nelson, the slave who had saved her. Cautiously advancing through the woods, she reached the Travis place. Climbing upon the gate-post, she saw two men at the house, and fainted from fright and exhaustion. These, Mr. Womac and Mr. Sam. Ellis, also saw her, and after they had revived her by pouring water in her face, Mr. Ellis[1] took her on his horse and carried her to Pate's Hill, where she found her husband's mother, but had little opportunity to rest from her trials and excitement.

People there were too much alarmed to allow anyone to rest. The least unusual occurrence was sufficient to produce the wildest confusion. A flock of sheep running

[1]These men lived near Pate's Hill, the former a school teacher for Mr. Joseph Claud at the Claud place, and the latter a planter on a portion of the farm now owned by Mr. William Leigh.

The Home of Mr. Richard Porter.

down the road was taken for the insurgents, and in a moment women and children, many of whom had collected at Pate's Hill, were flying to the swamps. Here they remained for two nights, sleeping upon the leaves of the forest and making use of the provisions hastily gathered as they rushed from their homes. This crowd proved more than Mrs. Francis could stand, so she decided to leave, declaring that she would rather die at the hands of the negroes than remain in such society. As she approached the country road she heard the sounds of horses' hoofs. Looking through the bushes, she recognized her husband as the third man of the company. Hearing her call, he went to her and took her, behind him, to Cross Keys and thence to her mother's home, near Seaboard, North Carolina, where she remained for some weeks nursing her sick mother.[1]

One mile from Mr. Francis', farther to the north, lay the home of Mr. Peter Edwards. This same division of the negroes now made their appearance here, to find that "old Jeff"[2] had assisted Mr. Edwards and his family to escape to the woods, where they were cared for by the slaves until all alarm was dispelled. Five of the slaves of this farm joined the insurgents. The rest were assembled after the departure of the raiders and the absentees

---

[1] She had heard the cries of her loved ones; had ridden twenty miles on horseback, besides having walked several; had spent several days and nights in the swamps, and was now nursing the sick. This was the experience of a woman who within a month brought forth her first born. How she survived it all was ever a wonder to her and still remains an example of what could be done by our ancestors. She lived, however, to tell the story of the crusade against the white inhabitants of her county and died only a few years since, leaving many children and grandchildren.

[2] His son, Hardie Musgrave, lives at Newsom's, Virginia, a hale and hearty old man of eighty summers, industrious and respected by all. He remembers Nat well, and says that the foregoing picture is the exact image of him. His master, Mr. Benjamin Edwards, did not live far from the Travis place.

were noted by Jeff and reported to his master. After the defeat of the gang these five returned home and were shot down in turn by the neighbors. Jeff, who had always been overseer, was now trusted more than ever for his faithfulness.

Previous to this time the insurgents seemed to be going from home to home without any aim as to final purpose and destination. But now, having drunk freely of apple brandy, mixed with gunpowder, and being extremely intoxicated, they took the main road to Jerusalem, the county seat. Capt. John T. Barrow lived three-quarters of a mile away. Mr. Nat Francis had sent him word that the British were coming, but not wishing to show any signs of concern in the presence of the negro messenger, Captain Barrow dismissed him very amicably. Mr. Drewry Bittle, a neighbor, had also brought the news that there was an insurrection of some kind. Captain Barrow had thus decided to flee to the home of his mother, who had married Capt. Newitt Harris, and he was waiting for his wife when the leaders of the band came in sight. Being very beautiful, and accustomed to dress very tastefully, she did not wish to appear beyond her home in her daily costume, and was making her usual preparations. Mr. Bittle was keeping watch for the negroes, but he did not have time to give the signal. Two or three negroes, seeing him, put spurs to their horses, and came near capturing him. However, casting aside his shoes, he safely reached the swamp, and they, unable to proceed farther, called to him, "Never mind, we will get you yet!" With some humor he replied, "Not today." Captain Barrow's lot was not to be so fortunate. The delay was fatal, and he perceived that it was useless to flee. The negroes were now within thirty yards of the dwelling. Taking his stand upon the porch, his pistol, rifle, and shotgun by his side, Barrow told his wife to fly for her life, while he fought for his home and his loved ones. It is said that she still

Home of Mr. Nathaniel Francis.

lingered and hindered his aim. But finally she fled, while
he held them at bay, first with his gun, pistol and rifle,
and, when these had been fired, with the butt end of his
gun, which he broke to pieces over their heads as they
forced him from the porch into the hall and thence into a
side room. He scorned to surrender and was not overcome until a window was raised and one of the band on
the outside, reaching in, cut his throat with a razor. Never
did man fight more desperately, and no hero should be
more honored than John Barrow. The insurgents recognized his bravery and drank his blood to make them
brave and determined. This was the only corpse respected.
Wrapping it in a bed-quilt, they placed it in the middle of the floor of his bedchamber with a plug of tobacco
upon his breast. When Nat was told the story of his
courage and resistance he said he was sorry such a man
had to be killed, and that the insurrection would not
have proceeded far if he had met this man in
the beginning. His resistance sufficed, however, to
save Mrs. Barrow. As she fled a negro girl, named
Lucy, seized her with the determination of holding
her for the rebels, but "Aunt" Easter came to the aid
of her mistress and fled with her to the woods, where they
found Captain Harris.[1] Mr. George Vaughan, brother of
Mrs. Barrow, was on his way to his sister's for a fox hunt.
Fortunately for the gang, he did not reach his brother-
in-law's house, or the result might have been more unfa-

---

[1] Mrs. Barrow was one of the principal witnesses against the
insurgents. She had seen them ride up to her home, and she
knew most of them, as they belonged to her neighbors. To one
who had yelled at her as she fled, "Never mind, we will catch
you yet," she remarked in court: "I know every one of you
scamps, as you belong to my neighbors." With a scornful grin,
however, the fellow replied, "No, it wasn't me." Her maiden
name was Mary Vaughan, daughter of Mrs. Rebecca Vaughan,
who was killed by the insurgents. She afterwards married a
Mr. Rose, and later a Mr. Moyler.

vorable for them. As they journeyed toward the next farm he was met and ruthlessly slain.

The farm of Captain Harris lay about a mile to the northwest. This gentleman had been a soldier in the War of 1812 and was now old and feeble. His large and prosperous farm was entrusted mostly to the care of the negro overseers, Aaron and Ben, who were also "stillers," and manufactured the apple brandy which caused much insubordination among the blacks. On Sunday Ben went to Dr. Jones' to visit his wife, and Monday morning while returning home he heard the report that the British were in the county killing the people. Most of Captain Harris' children were married, and his wife was in Sussex county visiting her daughter, having left the charge of the household affairs to "Aunt" Edie, Aaron's wife. Captain Harris would not believe Ben's story and refused to fly. This was very natural for a man of his intelligence. But Ben knew there was some danger afloat, and, with a heart full of love for his master, replied: "You shall go," and, taking the invalid upon his shoulders, bore him to the swamps behind the house.[1] Making him as comfortable as possible, Ben and Edie returned to look after the duties of the farm, and reached the house just as the negroes came in sight.

Two roads, one from the southeast and one from the southwest, meet at the lane gate and form the Barrow road.[2] Mrs. Robert Musgrave, the daughter of Capt. Harris, had been advised by a slave to flee to her father's, as the negroes had risen. George Musgrave, her husband's

[1] This place is owned by Mr. Samuel Drewry. A road now passes through the swamp.

[2] This road took its name from Captain J. T. Barrow, who constructed the greater part of it. It enters the Jerusalem and Cross Keys road at the Blackhead Sign-post, which is so named because the head of one of the insurgents who had been shot was cut off and stuck on it. It was ever afterwards painted black as a warning against any future outrage.

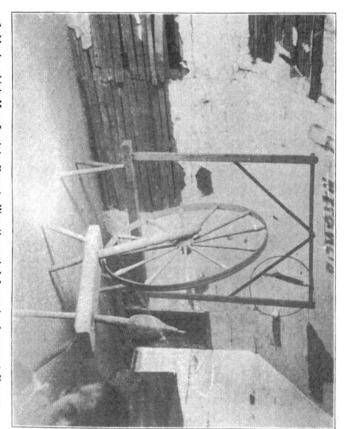

Cuddy in which Mrs. Lavinia Francis Was Concealed from the Insurgent Negroes.

brother, had also returned from school with the report about the British. Mrs. Musgrave's husband being away she took her twelve-months-old baby and this lad of ten upon her gig and went to her father's. She arrived from the southwest as the insurgents came from the southeast. Seeing her and the insurgents about the same time, Ben ran and told her to make through the house and close the door, so that the negroes could not see the direction she took. According to his orders, she had climbed over the garden fence and was proceeding down a corn row in search of her father, when she fainted, and but for the assistance of "Aunt" Edie, who came up with restoratives, she would have been caught. They could not find Captain Harris for some time and also were in danger of being betrayed by the cries of the baby, which was tired and thirsty. Mrs. Musgrave was afraid to be left alone, and, besides, feared betrayal. All the slaves had been trusted, and many of the ringleaders equally as much as this worthy woman. A want of confidence was natural. "Aunt" Edie realized this and did not blame her young mistress, but she saw the necessity of prompt action. Though not in theory, yet in practice, she was the mistress of the household. Stuffing a handkerchief in the child's mouth to prevent its crying, she set out in search of water, which was scarce in the woods in the month of August. But she was successful and soon returned with the water.[1] She had also found her master, whom they joined immediately.

The insurgents, however, had seen Mrs. Musgrave and asked Ben who it was. He told them, but said she was in the house in search of her parents, who had gone from home. Searching in vain, the negroes threatened to shoot Ben, but he insisted that she was in a cuddy. Thinking

[1] She is said to have found it in a cow's track and gave it to the child from a cup made of oak leaves.

this his last hope, and determined not to betray his people, he turned and ran. He saved his life, but was sprinkled with bird-shot. Ben and Aaron saved their people, and in addition supported the other slaves in their loyalty. Not one joined the insurgents, but, armed with pitch-forks and hoes, they prepared to defend their master if an attempt was made to find him. This was not the only test of Ben's loyalty. Soldiers came the next day in search of the negroes, and, thinking from his stammering that he wished to conceal them, they also threatened to shoot him. He again ran, to suffer the same fate as before. The insurgents having been routed at Dr. Blunt's on Tuesday morning, appeared the second time at Captain Harris'. They did not go to the house, as some soldiers were there. Aaron saw the negroes and told them that the "devil" was at the house and enough white people to eat them up. He then slipped to the house to report the facts, and a charge was made, which, as we shall see, completely ended the insurrection. He had been in the War of 1812 as Captain Harris' body servant, and when the negroes first appeared at his master's he tried to dissuade them from the plot, telling them that it was impossible, and that they had better return home, which fact they would realize if they had seen as many white people as he had seen in Norfolk. They would not heed his advice, but threatened to kill him. He replied that he was not afraid of them, and by his bold stand successfully defied their threats.[1]

[1] After this Ben and Aaron were complete despots in their own sphere. Everyone recognized their services and respected them. At his death Captain Harris left Aaron to the care of his son and Ben to Mrs. Musgrave—as it was she whom he had saved—with provisions that they were to do as they pleased and have all possible comforts. These instructions were faithfully obeyed. No one was too good to care for them. Three times a day the white children took Ben his meals, and when they did not suit him he would demand something else in the most authoritative tone. Of course, the children did not like this—they were too small to understand. But their mother knew too well what was

Mrs. Lavinia Francis.

Finding no victims, the insurgents began a search for money and other valuables, breaking open furniture, closets, and cellars for this purpose. The main object of their search—brandy—was found in abundance. Rolling the barrels into the yard and knocking out one end of each, they began their frolic. Nat had told this division he would bring up the other at Mr. Francis', but following the trail from there he found the work had been so speedily and thoroughly done that he was unable to overtake them until now. The negroes seemed to number about forty, some of whom were drinking, some loading their guns, and the greater part mounted and ready to start, when Nat and his division rode up. He was greeted with shouts and hurrahs, which only incited him to prompt action. It being between nine and ten o'clock, he gave the command to mount and march immediately. He placed the best armed and most trusted confederates in front, with orders to approach the houses as fast as they could ride for the purpose of carrying terror and devastation wherever they went, and also to prevent the escape of their victims and the spread of alarm. For this reason Nat never reached the scene of slaughter after leaving Mrs. Whitehead's, except in one case, until the murders had been committed, but he "got in sight in time to see the work of death completed, viewed in silent satisfaction the mangled bodies as they lay, and immediately started in quest of other victims."

In this manner the home of Mr. Levi Waller was vis-

---

due Ben, and when they complained of his bearing toward them she would always forbid any discourtesy and reply, "Remember where your mother would be if it had not been for him. He suffered his back to be shot for us." This was a fit recognition of the service of one of the truest of friends, and at the same time a lesson in morality, obedience, and respect, which these children remember to the present day. It cannot be said, then, that slaves were never honored nor received the recognition due them.

ited. It was about three miles from Captain Harris', and the center and general meeting place of the neighborhood. The boarding school there, of which Mr. William Crocker was principal, was well attended. The distillery, the blacksmith shop, and the wheelwright shop were other attractions for the neighbors. Many of the insurgents wished to turn to the left at Pond's shop and make for Major Humphrey Drewry's, who was noted for his excellent apple brandy. If their wishes had been obeyed the result might have been different. But Nat was making for Jerusalem, where he expected many reinforcements, arms, and ammunition. Thus they bore to the northeast just as Mrs. John Drewry, with her baby and nurse, came in sight. She was on her way to her brother's, Mr. Nat Francis, but the harness having broken, she stopped for her nurse to fix it, and the negroes passed on by the other road. Returning home, she spent several days in the woods, cared for by faithful slaves.[1]

It was nine or ten o'clock on Monday morning before any report of the insurrection reached Mr. Waller's, and the negroes were then within a few miles. It was here that the true nature of the plot was first discovered, it having been previously reported that the British were the perpetrators. Mr. Waller was at his "still" and the children at school, a quarter of a mile away, when some of the slaves reported to him that the negroes had risen and were on their way to his home. He sent to the school to report the news, and when the teacher appeared with the children Mr. Waller sent him to the house to load the guns. But before he could do so the insurgents arrived. Though several men and boys were here, they were forced to flee, being unarmed. Mr. Waller fled into the corner of the fence and was saved by his blacksmith, Davy, who

[1] "Aunt Jinnie" was the nurse, and "Uncle Sip," the negro who cared for Mrs. Drewry.

Hardie Musgrave.

ran in the opposite direction, yelling, "Here goes the old fox," thus drawing the blacks after him. Davy then returned and helped his master to escape to the plum orchard. Crocker[1] ran into the cornfield, pursued by a negro, and, stopping after he had gotten out of sight of the others, he dropped his unsheathed sword and prepared to shoot. But at that moment a little girl ran across the lane and the negro turned to pursue her. This little girl was Clarinda Jones, a girl of twelve years. She had tried to persuade her sister, Lucinda, to flee with her to the weeds, but when the latter decided to climb the kitchen chimney, Clarinda hid on the outside in a corner between the house and the chimney. Lucinda was discovered and killed. She clung so firmly to the sway-pole[2] that the flesh was torn from her fingers as she was dragged down. Alarmed by the fate of her elder sister, Clarinda ran just in time to attract the attention of the negro who was pursuing her teacher. As she mounted the fence the negro shot her. She fell, and though slightly wounded, she had the presence of mind to remain perfectly quiet, so that the darky did not discover her, though he rode so close that his horse ate of the weeds which concealed her. After his departure she crawled out and hid under an old shop and counted the blacks as they marched away to the next point of attack. She went to the swamp and was discovered there the next morning by men hunting for the insurgents. In response to their inquiries in regard to the manner of her escape, she said: "The Lord helped me." Taking her upon his horse, one

[1] Crocker's daughter, Mrs. Richard Stephenson, of Seaboard, North Carolina, owns the gold watch of her father, which he dropped as he was fleeing from the negroes, but which he stopped to pick up in order to leave no clue as to the direction which he took.

[2] This is a pole stretching across the chimney from which the cooking utensils were hung by means of the pot-hooks.

of these neighbors took her to her father, Mr. Burrel Jones.[1]

From the plum orchard Mr. Waller saw the movements of the negroes and heard the screams of his family and friends as they were murdered. Between ten and fifteen persons suffered death at this place. Many escaped, however, by concealing themselves in the weeds. Among them were Mr. Waller, two of his sons, and Mr. William Crocker, who finally made their way to Cross Keys. From there Mr. Waller proceeded to Murfreesboro, North Carolina, and communicated the news to the "Old North State," which immediately prepared for assistance. John H. Wheeler, the historian, says: "Well does the author remember the arrival of Levi Waller in Murfreesboro to tell the story of his family." Mrs. Waller had advised the men to flee, as she thought the negroes would not kill the women and children. How mistaken, poor woman! One of her own slaves slashed her with a razor as she defended herself. Martha Waller was concealed by the nurse under her large apron, but the child could not endure the reckless destruction of furniture, so arose and threatened to tell her father. One of the negroes seized her and dashed her

[1] Mr. Jones moved to Mississippi, but afterwards lived in Northampton county, North Carolina, not far from his old home. He had sufficient reason to make him dislike Southampton, and it cannot be attributed to a want of feeling if he had a prejudice against the negroes. After the dispersion of the insurgents he was guarding a captive, and was advised by a friend to kill the negro. He refused to do this, but cut the prisoner's heel-strings and left. His wife also, a few months later passing from one farm to another about sunset, was accosted by a runaway negro, who, in response to her inquiry as to who he was, replied: "Chief cook and bottle washer, secret keeper and bottle stopper!" The woods were surrounded and the fellow taken and punished. Clarinda married a Mr. Wall, of Northampton, North Carolina, where a large number of children now survive her, one of them bearing the name of Lucinda. Mrs. Wall died only a few years ago, carrying to the grave two buck-shot which she had received in the calf of her leg.

Site of the Home of Capt. John T. Burrow.

to death against the ground. Only two of Waller's slaves —Albert and "Yellow" Davy—took part in these depredations.

The band of insurgents had their number greatly swelled by forced recruits as well as by volunteers, so much so that when Nat gave the usual order, "Mount and march immediately," he had to compel several, who were trying to escape, to join him. All were further intoxicated at Mr. Waller's, and as they staggered along the road in the direction of the county seat, some fell from their horses and were left behind. Mr. Thomas Gray lived on this road. He had several sons and daughters, but they were not disturbed, which can be explained only by the fact that the insurgents had become insubordinate and careless from the effect of large amounts of intoxicants they had taken. Mr. William Williams, who lived three miles from Waller's shop, had been recently married and lived in a neat and comfortable little cottage near the road. He and two boys, Miles and Henry Johnson, were in the fodder-field, Mrs. Williams being at the house alone. The negroes appeared, asked her where her husband was, and gave her the choice of dying there or with him. She preferred the latter, but as they went in search of him she fled and was some distance from them, when she was pursued, overtaken, and made to get up behind one of their number and forced to view the mangled and lifeless bodies of her loved ones. Then, pillowing her head upon the bloody sod at her husband's side, she was shot to death.

Mr. Williams' uncle, Mr. Jacob Williams, was away from home early Monday morning, and when he returned, about eleven o'clock, he found Nelson, one of his slaves, and one of the principal instigators of the rebellion, dressed in his best clothes. Being in a hurry to go to the woods to measure timber for Mr. Drewry Simmons, Mr. Williams did not stop to investigate the overbearing manner of Nelson. A few days previous to this Nelson remarked to Mr. Caswell Worrell, Mr. Williams' overseer, that the white people might look out and take care of themselves, as something was going to happen before long which anyone of his practice could tell. He was a negro of bad character, and professed to have prophetic power, but such remarks had been so common with him, and the slaves in general were so contented, that no attention was paid to him and not the least suspicion of the insurrection was aroused until the blacks arrived, about twelve o'clock on Monday, the 22d of August. Nelson had been waiting for them. He went to the field where Mr. Worrell was superintending the field hands and got permission to go to the house, saying he was sick. He also persuaded the overseer to accompany him, thinking to deliver him into the hands of the insurgents, but Mr. Worrell escaped to the woods. Nelson was not very sick, however, when he saw his confederates aproaching. He was the leader in this section and seems to have worked faithfully for the cause. Going into the kitchen, he helped himself to the dinner then preparing, remarking to the cook: "Cynthia, you don't know me. I don't know when you will see me again," and then, stepping into the yard, walked over the mangled bodies of his mistress and her three children, who had been slain without the least manifestation of grief or pity. The other slaves of Mr. Williams were actuated by the spirit which filled the majority of the slaves of the county. Though Nelson was allowed the greatest freedom, liberty, and intercourse with them, and was a pretended leader or prophet, yet he was unable to persuade one of his master's servants to revolt. This is one of the most striking features of the insurrection. Even when all the whites of a family had been killed, the slaves remained faithful and gladly testified at the trials of the culprits. Any account of Southampton would be defective which failed to compliment

Elm Growing on the Grave of Capt. John T. Barrow.

the good sense, fidelity, and affection of the slaves on this occasion. It was only the deluded and fanatical who took part.

When the insurgents arrived at Mr. Williams' the first murder perpetrated was that of Mr. Edwin Drewry. He was overseer for Mr. James Bell, and had come, with Stephen, a slave of the latter, for a load of corn. They were trying to decide which should go for a measure, when, looking out of the crib, Mr. Drewry exclaimed, "Lord, who is that coming?" He ran, but was pursued, shot, and disemboweled. Stephen was made to mount his horse and join the company, but at his trial he was acquitted, for at Parker's field he escaped and rode into Jerusalem, hallooing at the top of his voice who he was and why he was riding so rapidly. This was to avoid alarming the people. Mr. Worrell lived a few hundred yards from the "great house," as the darkies call the residence of the landlord. After visiting this and killing his wife and two children, the insurgents came back for dinner to the home of Mr. Williams, who had just returned from the woods. He barely had time to view the bodies of his murdered family, when he was forced to flee to the corn-field, from which he could view the actions of the negroes and hear Nelson say, "Now, we will have the old fox."

Mrs. Rebecca Vaughan, a highly respected and hospitable widow, lived, with her two sons, a quarter of a mile northwest of Mr. Jacob Williams'. George had gone to his brother-in-law's for his sister and was expected to return with the fox hunters, who were to be entertained by his mother. The negroes were taken for these hunters and no attempt to escape was made. Mr. Arthur Vaughan, another son, and the overseer were murdered between the house and the "still." Proceeding to the house, the negroes found two defenseless women—Mrs. Vaughan[1] and Miss

[1] Her husband was Mr. Thomas Vaughan. This farm is now owned by the Myricks.

Anne Eliza, daughter of Mr. John T. Vaughan, who was visiting her aunt and was at this time upstairs. Hearing much talking below, she came down to see the meaning of it. She was murdered and her body thrown into the yard, to decay in the hot August sun. Thus perished a lovely young girl of eighteen, the beauty of the county. Her aunt asked to be allowed to pray. But she prayed too long, and after repeated oaths and threats, the negroes ascended the stairs and murdered her upon her knees, her blood staining the floor, upon which its traces may still be seen.

After feasting and partaking again of the famous and enticing Southampton fluid, the march was resumed. The negroes now numbered about sixty, armed with guns, axes, swords, clubs, and every conceivable form of weapon, and Nat determined to lead them directly to Jerusalem. He succeeded in persuading them to pass the homes of several poor white people, but the intoxication and licentiousness into which they had fallen proved too powerful for him. Passing the "Blackhead" sign-post, they turned to the left. The courthouse was only four miles away, but they were destined not to reach it. After advancing upon this road for three-quarters of a mile, they came to the lane gate which led to the dwelling[1] of Mr. James W. Parker. Nat wished to pass on, but his men desired to go up and enlist some of the servants, who had relatives among the insurgents. The subordinates prevailed. With seven or eight men, the leader remained at the gate, while their comrades proceeded to the house, which was half a mile away. Mr. Parker's servants were faithful, however, and remembered the thoughtfulness of their mistress,[2] who, in the midst of danger and excitement, took time to prepare rations for them, as she was

[1] This place now belongs to Mr. Willie Story, of Newsom's, Va.
[2] Her maiden name was Martha Vaughan. She was a sister of Mrs. Barrow and daughter of Mrs. Rebecca Vaughan.

Capt. Newit Harris' Brandy Cellar.

uncertain when she would return. Only three of them were brought to the bar of justice; one was acquitted and the other two were discharged without trial on the testimony of their master, that if they were guilty it was due to evil influences, and that they had hitherto been faithful and true. Nor did the band find any victims. Mr. Harry Vaughan, Mrs. Parker's uncle, had heard of their approach and warned his relatives to fly to the county seat. They barely escaped. Mrs. Parker returned for the little baby, which in the excitement had been left in the cradle, and she would certainly have been overtaken had not the negroes made a halt instead of obeying their leader.

The Parkers' cellar was well stored with Southampton brandy and all the necessaries of a typical Southern home, for Mr. Parker[1] was an industrious and prosperous farmer, and had accumulated much wealth previous to this unexpected occurrence. Barrels of brandy were rolled into the yard, poured into tubs, and sweetened with the best quality of loaf sugar. The blacks drank of this until the sugar was crusted upon their lips, and then lay down under the shade of the trees to slumber before returning to their leader. In the meantime Nat had become impatient and set out in search for them. He found them, some slumbering and others relating their bloody deeds. They were immediately ordered to march, as they had previously plundered the furniture in their search for money and other valuables.[2]

Retracing their steps, they were suddenly met by a body of white men. Captain Arthur Middleton was com-

[1] Mr. Parker moved to Tennessee after the insurrection. He, however, returned later and bought of Mr. James Trezevant the farm which Mr. Henry Ferguson now owns.

[2] It is difficult to explain why they took all the silver and left the gold, except by the fact that only the most ignorant and deluded slaves were connected with the plot, and they had never seen enough of the latter metal to know its value.

mander of the county militia and had collected about twenty men to resist the onslaught of the negroes. They reached Waller's soon after the blacks had left. Seeing the bodies of the victims, not yet cold in death, and one of them, a little girl,[1] still having life in it, Middleton told his men that he was going to return and look after his own family. Eighteen of them refused to return, and, under command of Captains Alexander P. Peete and James Bryant, followed the trail of the negroes, now more than fifty strong, until they were overtaken in Parker's Field.[2]

This band of eighteen whites, opening fire on those at the gate and dispersing them, advanced up the lane to meet the main body of the blacks, who knew nothing of what had happened and were expecting nothing of the kind. The negroes had traversed a distance of thirty miles without the least resistance, except that of a single man, and had committed nearly sixty murders. Yet it seems remarkable that they were not determined and that a band actuated by such purposes should have resisted so feebly the first opposition. It might be thought that mere desperation would have led to greater effort for defense. But upon discovering the whites, their brave spirits, due to want of forethought of the consequences, gave way and alarm seized them. Consequently, Nat

[1] Her body was removed from the sun and placed under a tree, but when Captain James Bryant returned it was lifeless.

[2] Soon after leaving Waller's these men found Albert, one of Mr. Waller's slaves, who had fallen from his horse in a fit of intoxication and was now making his way back home. They felt certain that he had joined the rebels, but to give him the benefit of the doubt as well as to avoid being burdened with a prisoner Sampson Reese cut his heel-strings. His master was binding up these wounds when the Greenesville Cavalry, under Dr. Scott, appeared. It very much incensed this gentleman to see a man binding up the wounds of one of the murderers of his own family when their bodies were still unburied. After a severe reprimand to the master, he ordered the negro to be tied to a tree and shot.

Site of Kitchen at Waller's (Showing the Sill of the Fireplace) and the Graveyard Where the Murdered Whites Lie Buried.

THE SOUTHAMPTON INSURRECTION.

thought it best to halt and take a defensive position. Captain Peete[1] ordered his men to reserve their fire until within thirty feet of the blacks. This order was obeyed until they were within one hundred yards, when Hartie Joyner,[2] who was second from the front, accidentally fired his gun and his horse rushed headlong into the midst of the negroes. One of the negroes was riding the mother of this horse, and this fact partially explains his headlong dash. Such confusion was caused among the advancing column that seven of the whites retreated. Thinking his men would take courage at this and that the whites had only fallen back to meet others with ammunition, Nat gave the command, "Fire, and, G— d—n them, rush!" The whites, however, were not disheartened, and ten of them stood their ground until the negroes were within fifty yards. They then fired and retreated. The blacks pursued them for two hundred yards, when, crossing a little hill, they discovered that the whites, reinforced by another party from Jerusalem, had halted and were reloading their guns. Two of the whites had been left upon the field, but they were only stunned. Captain Bryant had also narrowly escaped, his horse having become unmanageable. But several of the negroes being killed and the bravest wounded, the others became panic-stricken and scampered over the field. Seeing that his cause was defeated and that more men were coming up than he saw at first, Nat determined to go by a private road, crossing the Nottoway river at the Cypress bridge, three miles below Jerusalem, and to attack the place in the rear, as he knew he was expected to come over the

[1] For his bravery and cool bearing on this occasion he was commissioned, and qualified September 22, 1831, as colonel of cavalry in the Fourth Regiment, Second Brigade.

[2] He escaped to Jerusalem, but his horse was sprinkled with shot, and curiously every spot hit was afterward covered with grey hair.

Jerusalem bridge. This was his only hope, as his ammunition had almost given out.

The reinforcing party proved to be from Jerusalem and knew nothing of the party which had gone with Captain Peete. They had been told by Mr. Parker and his family that the negroes were in the field, and had just fastened their horses to await the return of the negroes to the road. Hearing the firing, they immediately rushed to the spot and arrived just in time to arrest the progress of the negroes and save the lives of their friends and fellow-citizens.[1] For the people of Jerusalem this was the most important battle on record. More than sixty victorious negroes were within three miles. At least four hundred women and children had assembled in the town and were guarded by only a few men, the rest having set out in pursuit of the enemy. If the blacks had succeeded in conquering the whites at Parker's Field they would have murdered these helpless creatures, gained arms, ammunition and recruits, and would have marched to the Dismal Swamp, where it would have been very difficult to subdue them. As it was, not a white man was lost. This was due to several causes. In the first place, the negroes fired over the heads of their enemy. Secondly, they were armed with few rifles, fowling-pieces loaded with bird-shot being the general weapons. The negroes were also in want of ammunition and used gravel for shot, Nat insisting that the Lord had revealed that sand would answer the same purpose as lead.[2] The militia, too, might have effected a complete destruction of the negroes if they had been prop-

---

[1] John Vaughan, transformed into a perfect dare-devil by the depredations made upon his relatives, three times shot the horse from under Hark, who remounted every time, Nat himself catching a horse that was running past and holding it for him.

[2] No doubt this was a device to prevent panic among his men. He thought he would reach Jerusalem before any very serious need would arise for ammunition, the axe and club in the meantime sufficing for weapons of execution.

Mrs. Clarinda Wall (nee Jones) and Husband.

THE SOUTHAMPTON INSURRECTION.   67

erly armed. But some time before the Legislature had modified the semi-annual drill and had called in the arms. Consequently the whites were also armed with shot-guns and insufficiently drilled. Nevertheless, the blacks had been sufficiently routed to render further depredations impossible. The majority fled to their homes and many escaped punishment by convincing their masters that they were not in the fight or that they had been forced to join the insurrectionists.[1]

Twenty, however, followed their leader toward Jerusalem, but after going a short distance on the private road they overtook several others, who told them that the rest were dispersed in every direction. They no doubt also learned that Cypress bridge was guarded. These facts did not discourage Nat. He had more of the spirit of desperation, and, after making in vain every effort to collect sufficient force to proceed to Jerusalem, he determined to return, as he was sure the negroes had deserted toward their old homes, where they would join him. He intended to raise new recruits and begin the raid anew, and he sent some of his men ahead to notify those who had returned to meet him on the Wednesday or Thursday following. Together with others, he proceeded to return by another route to Boykin's District, where most of the insurgents lived. Bending his course to the southwest, he visited the home of Mr. Sugars Bryant,[2] who fled as the blacks came in sight. All the whites had escaped and no more victims were found. It was now late in the afternoon and there had been sufficient time for the news to spread. Many of the slaves who had been forced to join the band

---

[1] One of them, terribly wounded, one arm having been shot off, came to Mr. Nat Francis a few days later and asked what duties he wished him to perform. Mr. Francis calmly replied that he would show him in a short time. So, taking him up behind his gig, he took him to the court house, had him tried and hung.

[2] Mr. J. L. Bishop now owns this place.

lagged behind and finally deserted to inform the whites of the danger.[1]

Mrs. John Thomas lived two miles to the southwest of Mr. Bryant's. This is one of the most beautiful and historic places in Virginia, surrounded by lovely oaks and spacious lawns. Such now is the home and birthplace of Gen. George H. Thomas, at this time a mere boy of fifteen years. Mr. James Gurley, a neighbor, was on the lookout for the negroes. Keeping at a distance, he moved along before them to warn the neighbors of their approach. It was he who rode up and told Mrs. Thomas that the insurgents had mistaken the main road and were approaching by one which led to the rear of the residence. Thus she drove out of the front gate just before the rebels appeared from the other direction. Fearing they might be overtaken if they continued in the road to Jerusalem, the Thomases abandoned the carriage and escaped on foot through the woods. The "stiller," seeing the insurgents coming, jumped over the well and hid in the bushes, where he could see and hear them as they assembled under his "still" shed. No plundering was done, and, as the family found the dwelling as they left it, it is probable that the insurgents simply insisted that the slaves should follow them. Forcing the family slaves to halter their horses and mount, Nat hastened on his way. Sam, the negro overseer, took his son Leonard with him, but whispered to him to slide quietly off the first chance he got and to tell his mother to get the keys, which he had hid in the cider-press loft, and look after the affairs of the farm in his absence. Sam also found a chance to escape, and, putting spurs to

[1] Among this number was a slave of Mrs. Gideon Bell. He related that his courage failed him in his determination to escape, but the brandy and powder which they gave him to incite him to desperation only inspired courage, and watching his chance he put spurs to the thorough-bred horse upon which he was riding, and, leaving his pursuers far behind, he spread far and wide intelligence of the movements of the blacks.

Old Shop at Waller's.

his horse, he rode to Jerusalem, followed by the other Thomas negroes, and reported to his mistress. For safe keeping they were lodged in jail that night, but were released the next morning without trial.

Mr. James Gurley saw the insurgents following a cart filled with women and children and reported the fact to Major Pitt Thomas.[1] Placing himself between the negroes and the cart, Major Thomas held them at bay until the lady, who proved to be Mrs. Barrett, and her children escaped to the home of her mother, Mrs. Lucy Gurley. This lady walked up and down her front porch, declaring, "I'll be dad if I am afraid of any negro who may come to my house." Fortunately the negroes did not come and she was saved, but her servants were not as brave as their mistress and fled to the corn-field.

Bearing around to the southwest, the darkies came to the Spencer place.[2] They broke open the door, but the family had fled to Cross Keys. With the same result they visited Mr. Henry Blows' and other places. Then, turning to the northwest, the negroes crossed the Barrow road and took the Belfield road. Walnut Hill was the first home on this road. Mr. Harry Vaughan, a bachelor, lived here, and, on hearing of the rising of the negroes, he assembled his servants and told them that they were at liberty to do as they liked, either to remain or to go with the insurgents. They chose the former course, and not one of them deserted, though their gate was passed as the band proceeded to Buckhorn, Major Thomas Ridley's Quarter, where they stopped to spend the night. Sterling Lanier, the overseer, jumped into the cotton patch and escaped. Four of the Ridley negroes joined the insurgents, who had again recruited to the number of forty. Two of the four—

[1] The commission of Major of Infantry in the Sixty-fifth Regiment was given him, and he qualified September 8, 1831. This was in recognition of his deeds on this occasion.
[2] Now owned by Mrs. Bettie Pope.

Curtis and Stephen—were sent off to make new recruits in the neighborhood of Newsom's and Allen's Quarter,[1] having been told by Nat that the whites were too much alarmed to make any resistance. But they soon discovered their delusion, were captured, and hanged.

Posting sentinels, Nat lay down to sleep for the night. But he was soon aroused by the signal of one of the sentinels, who reported that they were about to be attacked. He awoke and found a great stampede, some of his men mounted and others in great confusion. Some of the bravest were ordered to ride around and reconnoitre. On their return, the other men, not knowing who they were, became alarmed and fled, so that the number was again reduced to about twenty. It was now necessary to take active measures and to exert every effort to make a grand rally in the neighborhood from which they had started. So, marching at rapid speed, Nat led his men to the house of Dr. Simon Blunt,[2] who lived a mile and a quarter away. This gentleman was a positive but indulgent master. On the morning of the 22d, when he heard that the negroes had risen, he assembled his slaves and stated the facts of the case. True to his trust, he told them to take their choice—remain and defend him and his family or join the insurgents. The advice and warning of the master had its effect. His slaves had the utmost confidence in his words, and replied that they would die in his defense. There were only six guns, one more than enough for the whites, two men and three boys. So, arming themselves with grubbing-hoes, pitch-forks, and other farm implements, the slaves stationed themselves in the kitchen at the side of the house, while the whites protected the dwelling. Such mutual confidence is remarkable, slaves defending a white family and whites preferring their protection to that of a

[1] Now Sunbeam.
[2] Mr. Sugars Pope now owns "Belmont."

Home of Mrs. Rebecca Vaughan.

THE SOUTHAMPTON INSURRECTION.   71

body of their own race, who had fortified the home of Major Thomas Ridley, a few miles away, where the women and children of the neighborhood were assembled.[1] Nat did not expect to find any of the white people at home, and only intended to enlist the servants. The yard gate was locked and chained, and when one of the men tried to unlock it Nat remarked that he could not be stopped by a fence, and ordered the gate to be broken down. Hark[2] was the commander on this occasion. On riding through the yard, he fired a gun, to ascertain whether any of the family were at home, and immediately young Simon Blunt[3] and Futrell, the overseer, opened fire.[4] It was just

[1] Among those who had fled here were the wife and children of Mr. Robert Nicholson, who lived at the "Yellow House," the farm adjoining Dr. Blunt's. He was away from home, and his wife was undecided what to do when she was told by one of her servants that the negroes had risen. She feared betrayal to the insurgents, but the faithful old darky pleaded, and raising his hands with the utterance, "I declar' 'fore God dey is commin'," he persuaded her to follow him to Major Ridley's. Every moment the guard here assembled expected the arrival of the insurgents and resolved to die or conquer. So great was their indignation that it was all the ladies could do to save the nurse of Mrs. Nicholson from being thrown from the window when she remarked that she wished that they would come along, as she wished to see them fight. This expectation was not to be realized, however.

[2] Hark was the negro version of Hercules, and they also called him "General Moore," as he had originally belonged to Mr. Thomas Moore. Probably the name "Hark" was the more readily assumed from the fact that Hark Travis had heard of a famous negro general named "Hark," who served under Saood II., the leader of the Wahabees, the reforming Mohammedans of Arabia. This general, about 1810, carried his arms across the Euphrates and threatened Damascus.

[3] Commodore Elliott, of the United States steamer Natchez, rendered efficient aid in suppressing this insurrection, and he was much impressed with the bravery of young Blunt. The Richmond Compiler of September 8, says: "Elliott is a fine fellow. The good feeling he manifested by his prompt action in defense of Southampton has endeared him still more to me, as I am sure it will to every true-hearted Virginian." This was the man who related the story to President Jackson. The latter was so impressed with the account of the defense at Blunt's that he

before the break of day on the morning of August 23, and all night had the arrival of the negroes been awaited. Futrell was on the porch and the others on the inside. They had established a systematic mode of defense. Those on the inside, assisted by the women, were, in addition to firing, to load the guns and pass them out of the window to him, and after the rebels had been put to confusion the slaves were to rush out and make an attack. The gate was eighty yards from the house and the negroes entered cautiously until within twenty yards, when the gun was fired. This shot was fatal. The commander, Hark, fell at the first fire and crawled off into the cotton patch, where he was captured by the slaves.[1] One other was killed and several wounded and captured, but the rest of the negroes retreated in all directions, when the slaves rushed out and assisted most heartily in the repulse and taking of prisoners. It was one of them, Frank, who made the first capture.[2] This was the last stand made by

immediately commissioned Simon Blunt, a lad of fifteen, a midshipman in the United States Navy under Elliott's command. Blunt distinguished himself under such an efficient commander and rose to the office of lieutenant. Loved and esteemed by all, he died in Baltimore, April 27, 1854.

[4]Mr. W. N. Ragland, of Petersburg, owns a clock which belonged to Dr. Blunt, and which still has the shot embedded in it which was fired by the insurgents.

[1]He was dangerously wounded, and Dr. Blunt kept him for several days, nursing his wounds. He was then taken to the county jail, where every attention was paid him, his wounds dressed and the best of food given him. It is proverbial in the county how he cracked the chicken bones with his teeth. He was too valuable a witness, and it was necessary to have his testimony in the trials of his associates. It was in this helpless condition, the doctors feeling his pulse and propped up on pillows so he could see them, that he, at his own request, received the Thomas family, to whom he talked freely and remarked, "If you had been at home you would not be here now."

[2]His prisoner was Moses, who belonged to Mr. Thomas Barrow, and who, when within thirty feet of the house, dismounted and chased Mary, a negro girl, who, according to the instructions of her mistress, was fleeing with her little child. She ran into

Blackhead Sign Post.

the blacks. Nat determined to retrace the route he had taken the day before. But he was very much discouraged, as the people of his own color had turned against him.[1] He turned to the southwest and came to Captain Harris', where he had been the day before. In the woods near this place the Greenesville cavalry charged the few who still clung together and killed nearly all of them, among the killed being Will, the savage executioner.[2]

Two, however,—Jacob and Nat—remained faithful to their leader and, with him, concealed themselves in the swamp until nearly night, when Nat sent them in search of Henry, Sam, Nelson, and Hark, to direct them to rally their men at the Cabin Pond, the rendezvous of the preceding Sunday. He himself immediately retired thither. The next day he saw white men riding around in search of him. He then concluded that Jacob and Nat had been taken and compelled to betray him. They were taken, and, it is very likely, betrayed him, as the whites had discovered the place of general rendezvous, but they had also helped to encourage the fugitives and to circulate their leader's orders.[3] Nat was discouraged by the appearance of the white men on Wednesday and gave up all hope for the present. On Thursday night, supplying himself with

the garden and made the child hide in the bushes, while she returned to meet her pursuer. But Frank had seen the chase and followed Moses, who ran, shouting, "G—d d—n you, I have got you," and captured him, without the least resistance, in the corner of the fence.

[1] It is said he remarked, "We must turn to the north."

[2] For months skeletons could be seen in these woods.

[3] At the trial of Mr. Benjamin Edwards' negroes, two who had remained constant testified that on Tuesday, while the white people and some other slaves were at Waller's burying the dead, Thomas Haithcock, a free negro, and four boys came to Mr. Edwards' and stated that "General Nat" would be there on Wednesday or Thursday to enlist four "likely boys" belonging to this gentleman. These negroes confessed that they had been with the insurgents and intended to join them again, and persuaded three of these "likely boys" to consent to go with them.

provisions from Mr. Travis', he scratched a hole under a pile of fence rails in a field and concealed himself therein.[1] He knew that he was suspected of being concealed in the woods, so was careful to select a spot, elsewhere. Here he lay hid for six weeks, never venturing out except for a few minutes in the dead of night to get water, which, however, was very near.

The course traveled by the insurgents is somewhat roughly represented by the figure eight, and well characterizes their ideas and knowledge of the country, and shows a general want of aim, purpose, and discipline. Detachments visited the places lying within this boundary, as also those contiguous to its exterior, but no one was there murdered. The whites had been warned by loyal slaves and fled.[2]

PURSUIT AND CAPTURE OF THE INSURGENTS.—The resistance offered at Parker's Field and at Belmont was sufficient to completely quell the insurgents. For a day and night the negroes had traversed the country, leaving desolation in their

[1] This cave is on the farm now owned by Mr. Albert Francis.

[2] Many residences of important and distinguished citizens schools and churches lay within this space. Mr. John K. Williams was the principal of the school attended by the children of the neighborhood of Cross Keys, and he had assembled his pupils when it was announced that the negroes were making in the direction of his school, which was a short distance from the main road and about a mile from Mr. Nat Francis's. This man never recovered from the shock. He became almost insane from grief, and at Branch's Bridge, which is on the Virginia and Carolina line, and was consequently well guarded and a place of refuge, Mr. Williams wished to kill every negro who came in sight. It was with difficulty that he was restrained from killing a negro boy who had been sent to report the condition of affairs in the neighborhood of the riot. Mrs. Nathan Pope, of Newsom's, is the daughter of Mr. Williams.

"Turner's Old Meeting House," which claimed the membership of the majority of the murdered victims, stood within these bounds. This church still stands, and though its name is changed, bears witness to the days of August, 1831.

Residence of Mr. James Parker (Magistrate).

track, and had yet met with no resistance. This might lead to the supposition that the people of Southampton were ignorant, undisciplined, or cowardly. But such was not the explanation of Nat's success. No sign of rebellious spirit had appeared among the slaves, and the leaders had been especially industrious and obedient preceding the 21st of August. The citizens had been thrown completely off their guard. Many of them were attending the camp-meeting[1] in Gates county, North Carolina, whither had assembled people from all the neighboring counties of Virginia and North Carolina to spend some days in the accustomed manner of such religious meetings. Thirty miles from home, they could know nothing of what was going on. Monday morning a man rode at full speed into the camp, crying at the top of his voice: "The negroes are in a state of insurrection in Southampton county and are killing every white person from the cradle up, and are coming this way." No organized effort, under such circumstances, could be made. Each one thought first of his own home, and set out immediately to find his relatives, some murdered and others in the greatest state of confusion. Then, too, the commencement of the raid was in the dead of night, and the murderers, proceeding noiselessly from farm to farm, had spared none who might spread the alarm. When morning came no one was left but slaves, and they were threatened with their lives if any signs of loyalty to the whites were exhibited. Many of them had witnessed the great success of the insurgents and the lack of opposition. These circumstances gave a temporary security to the negroes. The servants who gave the alarm were members mostly of homes which had not yet been visited. Seeing the insurgents in time, they had rescued their owners before appearing among the blacks. Even those negroes who had

---

[1] Camp-meetings were not so frequent in this section after this.

been persuaded or forced to join the band, and who afterward became disheartened, were afraid to report the true nature of the insurrection, and said the British were the offenders. The white people would more readily believe this than that their slaves were guilty. This report likewise reached the neighboring counties, where some of the negroes signified their desire to join the British in killing the whites. The Greenesville cavalry, on its way to the scene of the massacre, was met by some women and children fleeing to Belfield. Taking the cavalry for a body of the British, they fled precipitately. Not until nine or ten o'clock on Monday was it fully and generally ascertained that the slaves had risen. There was, as in all Virginia counties, a local militia, but it was difficult to assemble it quickly. The members lived some distance apart, and each naturally thought of the safety of his family before answering the summons to assemble at Jerusalem. Consequently, it was Tuesday before the regiment could be mustered. Still a small force had assembled on Monday, and it was this body that came to the rescue of the eighteen whites at Parker's Field.

On account of the first report that the British were in the county, and afterward, when the number of slaves was so exaggerated, the people thought it best to fortify the principal rivers and roads to prevent the spread of the insurrection into other counties of Virginia and North Carolina. They knew that the enemy were between the Blackwater, the Nottoway, the Chowan, and Meherrin rivers. Consequently, Cross Keys, Branch's bridge, Boykin's bridge, Haley's bridge, Belfield, Cary's bridge, and other places were fortified and made rendezvous for the women and children. This done, a small squad was left to protect the helpless, and the rest set out in search of the rebellious blacks. The young men and those who had no families assembled first, many being drafted as they were met. The men east of Nottoway river col-

Parker's Gate.

Battlefield in Parker's Field.

THE SOUTHAMPTON INSURRECTION. 77

lected the women and children under a sufficient guard at such places as Vicksville before rendering aid to the citizens of West Southampton. Ample assistance was afterward offered, but the riot had been practically suppressed by the Southampton militia and patrol before the knowledge of it had reached to any distance.

There were no ready means of communication, and the soldiers had to make their way up the navigable rivers to the nearest points and then on foot over the country roads to the scene of action. Consequently, it took some time for assistance to arrive, though lines of communication were estabilshed by means of couriers traveling from Jerusalem to Petersburg, Richmond, Smithfield, Suffolk, Norfolk, Murfreesboro, and other places of importance.[1] Such exaggerated reports, too, were in circulation that the distant militia had to look to the security of their own sections before leaving home.[2] Such was the excitement in Richmond and its vicinity that patrols were established in every section, and no one could enter a district after dark without danger of being killed or arrested, under suspicion of inciting rebellion among the slaves.[3]

---

[1] It is said that Mr. Thomas Jones killed two horses in carrying the report of the trouble to the Governor.

[2] The report was that the insurgents numbered one hundred and fifty mounted and the same number on foot, all armed with clubs, axes, scythes, fowling-pieces, and had killed sixty or seventy people. The battle at Parker's Field was said to have amounted to only a defeat of the blacks, in which but six were killed, eight wounded and the rest of the above number left to make their way to South Quay and probably to the Dismal Swamp. As late as the 23d it was reported in Richmond that seventy whites had been killed, and the militia in a body of three hundred, the powder with which they loaded their shot-guns having been ruined, as reported, by a shower of rain, were retreating before six or eight hundred negroes.

[3] Mr. John C. Stanard, of Roxbury, Spottsylvania county, on Monday evening, when the news of the insurrection reached Richmond, was in the city and intended leaving that night. He came by private conveyance, as there were no railroads. He had to hasten away before guards were stationed to prevent the

Gen. W. H. Brodnax, who had retired to Greenesville county to take command of the forces there, and with whom General Eppes had established communication, wrote the Governor, on the 25th: "The consternation unfortunately was not confined to the county where the danger existed, but extended over all immediately about it. Not a white family in many neighborhoods remained at home, and many went to other counties, and the rest assembled at different points in considerable numbers for mutual protection. In numerous instances females, with their children, fled in the night with but one imperfect dress and no provisions. I found every hovel at Hicks' Ford literally filled with women and children, with no way to lodge but in heaps on the floors, without an article of food or the means of procuring or cooking provisions. Other engagements of primary necessity prevented any attempt to ascertain their numbers. The charity of the few residents of the village would have been greatly inadequate to their support, and many seemed willing to encounter starvation itself rather than return home unprotected and while their husbands and sons were in the field." In Mecklenburg county the committee of safety wrote the Governor as follows: "Properly armed, we have entire confidence in our ability to defend ourselves, as well as to give aid to other places which may be threatened. Up to this time (August 25) there has been no insurrection or movement in this county, but we cannot expect forbearance if the insurgents below us are

passage of citizens. When he reached Merry Oak Tavern, in Hanover county, it was closed. After repeated knocking and banging at the door, someone poked his head out from a garret window and yelled that no one could get in there that night. Riding on, he was charged upon by a body of patrol, who thought at first that he was a negro and afterwards an accomplice. He, too, had taken them for negroes. But having convinced them of his true character he was released. It was, however, late in the night before he secured a resting place.—W. G. Stanard, Secretary of the Virginia Historical Society.

Bridge Over the Nottoway River at Jerusalem.

not speedily quelled. We consider that less time will be lost by Your Excellency's pressing or otherwise procuring wagons to transport arms hither." This expresses the state of affairs in a county whose inhabitants consisted of eight thousand whites and twelve thousand blacks. In Greenesville county the negroes, several hundred strong, were reported to be in communication with those of North Carolina and to be marching to the assistance of the insurgents of Southampton, and videttes were established between Hicks' Ford and Lawrenceville, Brunswick county.

Nor was the excitement and exaggeration less in Southampton. The people fled to North Carolina and the neighboring counties, or collected at the public places under guard. A citizen[1] says: "I recollect some of the incidents with as much vividness as if they had occurred only yesterday; the arrival of my Aunt Pierre at our farm from her abode a mile distant—the meeting took place at a well on our farm—she had in her hand a bag of bank notes, for my uncle was a capitalist—she burst into tears on meeting my mother, and lamentations by both and cries of distress were heard. It was but natural. All the families for some miles around assembled at Vicksville, a mile from our farm; a number of men guarded them, while a still more numerous body went together in search of the negroes who had risen in rebellion. We were in Vicksville some days; I know I slept on the floor, and the firing of shotguns was almost incessant."

The same excitement prevailed in North Carolina, and the people rushed to the county seats and little villages for protection. "It was 'court week,'" says John Wheeler, of Murfreesboro,[2] "and most of our men were twelve miles away, in Winton. Fear was seen in every face; women

[1] W. O. Denegre, St. Paul, Minn.
[2] Baltimore Gazette.

pale and terror-stricken, children crying for protection, men fearful and full of foreboding, but determined to be ready for the worst." The alarm was given by a "lily-livered boy," who rode post haste into town, that a hostile force was within eight miles. This report caused the greatest consternation. A respectable and aged gentleman, Mr. Thomas Weston, was so disturbed that he died of excitement. The citizens immediately formed a company and set out to meet the enemy, but the report proved false.[1] Such was the state of things in all the other counties. A citizen[2] of Northampton county, North Carolina, says: "One of the most memorable years in the history of Northampton county was the year of 1831, the year of Nat Turner's Southampton insurrection, which occurred in August of that year. Railroads and telegraphs were then unknown; couriers and fast horses supplied their places. The day after the insurrection over night, couriers were sent in every direction to notify the people. Northampton county, on Roanoke river, was the central point of attraction. Several thousand negroes were known to be on the great river plantations between Weldon and the line of Bertie county. Some of the negroes who had been captured in Southampton with arms in their hands had stated that the uprising on Roanoke was to have been simultaneous with that in Southampton, but that the mistake of a week in point of time had prevented it. The Johnsons, Longs, Amises, Lockharts, Exums, Pollocks, and others owned thousands of negroes on their extensive plantations on the river. The news left the impression on the minds of many that the Roanoke negroes would rise at the appointed time, which was just one week after the Southampton insurrection. The whole country

[1] A citizen of Murfreesboro, in Norfolk Herald, first Saturday in September, 1831.
[2] Col. D. H. Hardee, in Patron and Gleanor, Rich Square, North Carolina.

Cypress Bridge Over the Nottoway River.

was thrown into the greatest consternation. Almost every day some reports were started which produced great alarm. Many horses were killed by the couriers from rapid riding carrying the latest news from point to point. One courier from the river plantations brought the news to Jackson that five hundred negroes from Pollock's plantation were within six miles of Jackson. Other alarming reports were hourly coming in. In Gumberry, where my father lived, three or four families would meet together at a neighbor's house for mutual protection." A letter from Halifax, North Carolina, dated August 24, says: "I want you to send me, per the first boat, two kegs of gunpowder. The negroes have risen against the white people and the whole country is in an uproar. We have to keep guard night and day. We have had no battle yet, but it is expected every hour."[1]

It was natural, under the circumstances, that homes should be well fortified and guarded before any assistance was sent to the people of Southampton. This having been done, forces poured in from all directions, so that by Thursday, the 25th, there were three thousand troops on the way to Southampton and more preparing to set out. Richmond lies about eighty miles to the north of Southampton, but a courier had made his way thither by Monday night. The Governor immediately took prompt and efficient means to render assistance. He called out the militia of all the eastern counties and forced into service all the horses and wagons convenient to bear arms and ammunition to the scene. Eight hundred stand of arms were sent for the militia of Nansemond, Isle of Wight, and Surry counties, besides those sent to Southampton and to the other counties of Virginia. After a temporary company of cavalry had been formed for home protection

[1] Norfolk Beacon, Saturday, August 27, 1831.

and a force provided for nightly patrol, the two volunteer companies of Richmond—the Light Dragoons, under Captain Randolph Harrison, and the Lafayette Artillery, under Captain John B. Richardson—left for the scene of action. The former left at 5 o'clock on Tuesday, to travel the country road, and reached Southampton on Wednesday night; the latter, with four field pieces, embarked upon the steamboat Norfolk, to land at Smithfield, at which place they arrived, with one thousand stand of arms, on Thursday.

A gentleman, riding from Suffolk, reported the uprising in Southampton to the people of Norfolk on Tuesday morning. The authorities of Norfolk immediately appealed, through Captain Capron, of the Norfolk Independent Volunteers, to Colonel House, who was at the time in command at Fortress Monroe. At 6 o'clock on Wednesday morning Colonel House embarked on board the steamer Hampton, with three companies of soldiers and a piece of artillery. Colonel House, however, turned over the command to Colonel Worth and Major Kirby, who were reinforced in Hampton Roads by detachments from the United States ships Warren and Natchez. These detachments were commanded by Commodore Elliott, who, though just from a long cruise, insisted on going in person to the scene of action. This force of nearly three hundred men landed at Suffolk and marched to Southampton, which they reached Saturday evening and left Sunday at 2 p. m. The Norfolk Junior Volunteers, under Lieutenant Newton, and the Portsmouth Greys, under Captain Watts, left Thursday morning on the steamboat Constitution for Smithfield, where, on Friday, they were met by the Richmond Artillery as they were returning home. The Norfolk and Portsmouth companies consequently reversed their course. The citizens of Norfolk and Portsmouth also accoutred, formed themselves into companies of cavalry and set out to aid their fellow

Ridley's Quarters.

THE SOUTHAMPTON INSURRECTION. 83

citizens. Commodore Warrington, at the request of the civil authorities of Norfolk, forwarded from the Gosport Navy Yard muskets, pistols, swords, and ammunition, to be sent by way of Suffolk to the citizens of Southampton.

The Sussex regiment, four companies from Petersburg, and one from Prince George, under Captain Edward Ruffin, marched for Southampton. In addition to these, General Brodnax held the Brunswick and Greenesville militia, together with a fine troop of cavalry from Mecklenburg, ready to lend assistance at any moment. The Isle of Wight, Nansemond, and Surry troops were guarding the borders of the counties to prevent an escape of the insurgents to the Dismal Swamp. Their citizens also did active service in furnishing horses and carts for the transportation of the above-mentioned arms and ammunition from Smithfield and Suffolk to Southampton, as well as in providing couriers for carrying news.[1]

North Carolina, too, gave generous and ready aid. Hertford county proceeded to fortify her bridges, ferries, and villages, and, this accomplished, troops hastened to Southampton. Winton, the county seat, retaining a guard of seventy-five men, armed and equipped sixty others and sent them to the scene of insurrection, while Murfreesboro sent one hundred, between two and three hundred having been left to protect her inhabitants. The Northampton militia actually reached Southampton and the Gates militia was called out and ready to march at the first summons. The Roanoke Blues, of Halifax county, commanded by Colonel Jesse H. Simmons, reached Virginia Tuesday evening, while the rest of her militia, under Colonel Johnson, was held in readiness in case of an emergency. Couriers were passing to and fro to notify them in case they were needed and to keep the Carolinians

---

[1] The Legislature of the succeeding winter rewarded many of these citizens for the losses they had experienced on this account.

84   THE SOUTHAMPTON INSURRECTION.

informed of the state of affairs. The militia of many of the counties of Virginia, Maryland, and North Carolina were called out and held in readiness to suppress any attempt at servile insurrection. General Eppes, of Sussex county, was in command of the eastern division of Virginia, and consequently all forces reported to him.

The Southampton militia and citizens had fought well, had dispersed the rebels, and captured or killed all of them by Thursday except Nat Turner. But they were greatly assisted in the capture by the cavalry troops from abroad. Southampton was deficient in cavalry, which was especially needed. Consequently, many of the troops of cavalry remained, while the infantry returned,[1] in obedience to the general orders of General Eppes, issued on Wednesday, the 24th, which said the scene of the massacre was perfectly quiet and no more troops were needed. In a letter of the same date to the Governor he stated that all the insurgents had either been killed or captured except the leader.[2]

The condition of affairs in Southampton for about ten days after the massacre is best described by a committee of citizens in a letter to President Jackson, on the 29th of August, of which the following is an extract: "Most of the havoc has been confined to a limited section of our county, but so inhuman has been the butchery, so indiscriminate the carnage, that the tomahawk and scalping knife have now no horrors. Along the road traveled by

[1] One of the Norfolk volunteers wrote on Friday, August 27: "We succeeded in taking twelve men and one woman prisoner who, it appeared, had taken part in the massacre of the inhabitants of this county, together with the celebrated Nelson, frequently called by the blacks General Nelson. * * * In fact, all the ringleaders, with the exception of the prophet, have been taken or killed. Several of those who have been taken prisoners have confessed partly to the murder."—Norfolk Beacon.

[2] It appears from this that the report was true that Nat told his men at Blunt's that he was going to look out for himself and that they must do the same.

Residence of Dr. Simon Blunt ("Belmont.")

our rebellious blacks, comprising a distance of something like twenty-seven miles, no white soul now lives to tell how fiendlike was their purpose. In the bosom of almost every family this enemy still exists. Our homes, those near the scenes of havoc, as well as others more remote, have all been deserted and our families gathered together and guarded at public places in the county; and, still further, the excitement is so great that were the justices to pronounce a slave innocent, we fear a mob would be the consequence." Consequently, many rebels were shot, and some innocent negroes suffered.[1] Some prisoners taken near Cross Keys were shot by the Murfreesboro troops, under Mr. John Wheeler.[2] The heads of these negroes were stuck up on poles, and for weeks their grinning skulls remained, a warning to all who should undertake a similar plot. With the same purpose, the captain of the marines, as they marched through Vicksville on their way home, bore upon his sword the head of a rebel. The following is from the Norfolk Herald of August 29th: "Our Winton friend says, report says four of the desperadoes were preachers, and the one who commanded at the battle was a preacher, and assisted in murdering his mistress (Mrs. Whitehead). After they were dispersed this rascal returned home and pleaded that he was forced by the others. Ten of the mounted men from this county called at Whitehead's to see the horrors that had been

[1] It is said that some citizens who had been on Tuesday in search of rebels stopped at the Turner place for the night. Next morning a negro servant, while getting the saddles to harness the horses, was taken for a rebel and shot dead by Mr. Howell Harris, who was suddenly aroused from his sleep.

[2] He was father of the historian, John H. Wheeler. Mr. Francis entered the old store house at Cross Keys, where several prisoners were confined, and catching sight of Easter, who had saved his wife, embraced her with tears in his eyes and caused her immediate release. But, beholding Charlotte, he dragged her out, tied her to an oak tree, and she was riddled with bullets, he firing the first shot. The tree died from the number of shot which pierced it.

committed there, when this fellow came out, meeting them with smiles, and commenced telling them how roughly the negroes had also treated him. Some Southampton gentlemen who were with them as guides told them that he commanded the group at Parker's old field, when they all fired on him and he fell dead near the remains of his mistress."[1]

But, considering that Southampton was the scene of the massacre, her citizens did not commit as many errors as did those of other counties. General Eppes, in an official letter, dated August 31, noting the apprehension which prevailed among the negroes, said: "Coupled with the violence done upon some in the neighborhood, who had been shot at sight, even without knowing who they were, it does not seem to me remarkable that they should be under apprehension." But, referring to a case in a neighboring county, where a negro had been examined, discharged, and afterward shot, he adds: "I put an end to this inhuman butchery in two days, dispersed the troops from where they were assembled: the citizens retired, and I have not heard of an act of violence since, except upon the rebels in arms who refused to surrender." There was far less of this indiscriminate murder than might have been expected, and as many guilty negroes escaped as innocent ones perished. Two of the negroes of Mr. James Parker were discharged on his evidence that they had previously been of good character and that if they were guilty it was due to evil persuasion. They were sent South, however. Some years later Mr. Parker saw an account of the execution of a negro in Mississippi for attempted insurrection and rebellion. On the gallows he gave his name and confessed that he formerly belonged to Mr. James W. Parker, of Virginia, and had been sent

---

[1] This fellow probably commanded the group dispersed at Parker's gate.

Turner's Methodist Church.
(Now called Clarksbury.)

THE SOUTHAMPTON INSURRECTION. 87

thither for a crime similar to the one for which he was about to atone.

Mr. Henry DeBerry lived in Northampton county, North Carolina, about thirty miles from Cross Keys. Mrs. DeBerry, her fourteen-months-old infant and nurse, accompanied by two lady friends, were at the camp-meeting in Gates county when it was reported that the negroes were in a state of rebellion in Southampton. In the wild and hurried excitement, Mrs. DeBerry did not notice the route her driver had taken, having perfect confidence in him, until she met four men, who told her she had taken the wrong road and was within a few miles of the scene of the insurrection. The driver insisted he was going the right way, but on the appearance of Mr. DeBerry, who had heard of the insurrection and started in search of his wife, the negro admitted that he intended to carry the ladies to Nat Turner, kill them, take the horses and join the insurgents. Only the pleadings of his wife and these gentlemen restrained Mr. DeBerry in his determination to kill the negro. He was sent South and about twenty years ago the children of the family received a letter from this former slave, who was then in Louisiana, desiring to know about the family. He said: "For fear the old people are dead and the young ones will not recognize me, I am Otie, the carriage driver, who attempted to carry my kind and good mistress to old Nat Turner's insurrection." Many other negroes escaped through the charity of their owners or the reason and protection of some influential person. Major Pitt Thomas prevented the murder of several prisoners at Cross Keys by stepping between the negroes and those about to shoot, and saying it was time for such things to stop, and that the prisoners should be treated well and have fair trials. Colonel W. C. Parker, who had served in the War of 1812 on the Canadian border, and who was at this time a distinguished lawyer of Jerusalem, persuaded the people to spare the prisoners in the jail. Colonel Parker had also commanded a party of thirty or forty men who took part in capturing the insurgents.

It was through the influence of such men that confidence was restored and the citizens returned to their homes. General Eppes wrote the Governor on the 24th that the affair had been exaggerated, and that twenty resolute men could at any time have overcome the insurgents. General Brodnax substantiated this evidence in a letter dated the 25th, in which he said to the Governor he had dismissed the Sixty-sixth and Ninety-sixth Regiments, of Brunswick, who, with the Greenesville militia and a body of cavalry from Mecklenburg, had assembled at the first alarm, and that so completely had the people been convinced of the futility of the alarm that they had returned home from Hicks' Ford.

But the citizens could not be entirely at case. The leader of the insurgents was still at large. For weeks he lay in his cave, though diligently hunted, and it is said men rode over him in their search. Not only were the people of Southampton active, but all Virginia, as well as Maryland and North Carolina, exerted every effort to effect his capture. In September the Governor of Virginia issued a proclamation offering a reward of five hundred dollars for the capture of Nat, and urged the people to use their best efforts for his apprehension, that he might be dealt with as the law directed.[1] Southampton county also offered a reward of five hundred dollars, besides one of several hundred dollars offered by individual citizens.

Every suspicious character was taken for the fugitive. Consequently, the Governor received letters on different occasions announcing that he had been caught. The Norfolk Herald of October 1st said: "A young man from Jerusalem reported at Smithfield that Nat was captured

---

[1] National Gazette, September 21, 1831.

in some weeds on Nottoway river; that, when a body of horsemen appeared he ran and hid himself, but sank so deep in the mud that he was captured and put in the county jail. He also reported that Nat was well armed with a musket, two pistols, a sword, and a dirk, but that he did not fire a shot."[1] There was a report from Botetourt that a very suspicious character was met on the road between Fincastle and Sweet Springs, near Price's Tavern, by two young white men, who, while disputing over his dirk, let him run off, leaving his package behind. Some free negroes a few days later told Mr. Price that they had seen this same man, and that they were going with him to Ohio. The ferryman on New river reported that the man tried to cross over, and, when refused passage, ran off down the river.[2] It was also reported that Nat had been captured in Baltimore, Maryland. These reports continued until the people thought he had escaped either to Ohio or the West Indies, and began to subside into quietude once more. But at no time had he been five miles from the scene of the massacre. After remaining in his cave[3] for six weeks without leaving except for water in the dead of night, he became bolder, and concluded he could venture out. Consequently, he spent the day in sleep and the night in eavesdropping at the houses in the neighborhood, seeking information regarding the trials, etc., and returning before morning. Nat continued this course for a fortnight without gaining any information, and, fearing to speak to any human being, he might

[1] This resembles the true story of his capture, but it was a month later before he was captured.

[2] Norfolk Herald, September 28, 1831. This negro proved to be a Methodist preacher. He was dressed in a blue-cloth coat, and in his hymn-book was written "Mesheck Turner." In another place was "richman Wheeler," in child or negro writing, supposed to stand for Richmond Wheeler.

[3] This was not a natural cave, but a simple hole dug in the ground and covered with fence rails.

have continued it for some time had he not accidentally discovered.[1] "Red" Nelson, as we have seen, was allowed many liberties. Passing near Nat's cave one night when he was out, Nelson's dog entered and stole some meat. A few nights afterward Nelson and a friend were again out hunting and their dog entered the cave a second time. This time Nat was on the outside walking around, and the dog, on emerging, saw him and barked. Convinced that he was discovered, Nat spoke to the negroes, told them who he was, and begged them to conceal him. But as he was armed, they fled and reported the fact to the civil authorities. Immediately a body of citizens armed themselves and set out in pursuit. But he had moved. For the next fortnight he had many narrow escapes, and was several times seen by whites as well as by blacks. He seems to have lost all hope and to have had no definite place of concealment. He meditated surrender. One night Mrs. Lavinia Francis and her mother heard a knock at their door. They were afraid to wake Mr. Francis for fear of his being murdered in the manner in which his brother had been. Receiving no response, the intruder left. Nat afterward confessed he was the person, and said he came to surrender to Mr. Francis,[2] who, he believed, would be more merciful to him than anyone else. He also started for Jerusalem for this purpose and got within a few miles of the place, but his heart failed him. He then meditated getting out of the country, but as he could not travel by day and the patrols were so vigilant by night, this was impossible. He continued to roam from place to place, his chief place of concealment

[1] He kept an accurate account of the time by means of a notched stick, which was found in the cave at the time of his capture.

[2] Mr. Francis was a Christian and active member of Turner's Methodist Church.

Nat Turner's Cave.

THE SOUTHAMPTON INSURRECTION.

being a fodder stack[1] on Mr. Nathaniel Francis' farm. Here he was seen a few days before his capture by Mr. Francis, who shot at him as he ran, but he chanced to fall at the discharge and the contents of the pistol only penetrated his hat.[2]

This was October 27th, the Thursday before his capture. Men scoured the woods in the neighborhood, but he was not captured until Sunday morning, the 30th of October. He had been seen twice in an open field, so he concluded to move to the woods. Going about two miles to the northwest, he dug a cave[3] under the top of a fallen

[1] In eastern Virginia and North Carolina the blades of fodder are stripped from the cornstalks, cured, and tied into large bundles, and then firmly packed around a pole into a tall stack. Then the upper parts of the stalks, called the tops, with five or six blades of fodder on each, are cut and stacked near the fodder in a V-shaped heap, somewhat resembling a Gypsy tent, leaving a space beneath. It was here that Nat was concealed.

[2] He wore this hat at the time of his capture and exhibited it with much pride.

[3] This cave is like the first and is between one and two miles distant from it. It was dug with a fine dress sword, which has an ivory handle and is tipped with silver, and which was used by Nat in the massacre. It is now in the possession of Mr. James D. Westbrook, of Drewryville, Virginia, a relative of Mr. Phipps. The cave may still be seen on the farm of Mr. J. S. Musgrave, marked by the remains of a large pine, which stood at its entrance and which bears three gashes, cut by Mr. Phipps with Nat's sword.

Mr. Frank Alford, of Suffolk, claims to have Nat Turner's sword and musket, which his father, who was a member of the Portsmouth Cavalry, captured at Southampton. But Nat was not captured until two months after the return of the cavalry. Besides, Nat does not appear to have been armed with any weapon but a sword. Capt. J. J. Darden, who remembers the insurrection and has handled Nat's sword, says, in the Suffolk Herald:

"In your issue of July 14, 1899, appeared an item stating that the sword of Nat Turner, leader of the negro insurrection which occurred in Southampton county in 1831, was in the possession of Mr. Frank Alford, of Suffolk, whose father was a member of Captain Day's Portsmouth company that captured Nat.

"I wish to say that if Mr. Alford has Nat Turner's sword it must have come from Mr. James D. Westbrook, of this county,

tree and covered it with pine brush. Mr. Benjamin Phipps,[1] a poor but highly respected, hospitable and industrious citizen, was on this Sunday making his way to the home of a neighbor, and, as was the general custom for the last two months, had his gun with him. He does not appear to have been on the hunt. A squad of men on the search, however, passed through the woods just ahead of him, and he had taken a seat by a large tree to rest. Thinking all had passed, Nat poked his head out among

who owned it up to a few years ago, to my certain knowledge. A cavalry company from Norfolk or Portsmouth came to this county, but they did not capture Nat, for he was not caught for some two or three months.

"The insurrection collapsed at the residence of Dr. Blunt, the place where Mr. R. S. Pope now lives, near Pope station, on the Atlantic and Danville Railroad. Dr. Blunt's negroes told him that they were going to fight for him, and he directed them to get their axes and grubbing hoes and stay in his yard. (Negroes were not allowed to have firearms of any kind.) The insurrectionists reached Dr. Blunt's about sunrise, and when in his yard, half-way from the gate to the house, the whites upstairs opened fire and hit some of them, but did not kill anyone. Nat, seeing Dr. Blunt's negroes ready to fight, told his men that as the negroes and whites were all against them he should leave and shift for himself, and they could do the same. There were only about eight whites in the house. Dr. Blunt had a son sixteen years old, who displayed great bravery, for which he was made a midshipman in the United States Navy. He has been dead many years.

"Nat went off and dug a cave in the ground, but after awhile he found that a dog had discovered his hiding-place. He then went to the neighborhood where he was raised and dug another cave on the land of Dr. Musgrave, my wife's father. The neighbors got up parties and went through the woods hunting for him. The last time they went to look for Nat they scattered through the woods, and finally a man named Benjamin Phipps found the cave. He called for the others, and stuck his gun through the top covering and told Nat to throw out everything he had or he would kill him, and Nat threw out his gun and sword. I do not believe that Nat made the sword. Mr. Benjamin Phipps certainly found Nat and captured him.

"I do not write this thinking you knew you were publishing what was not true, but only to correct a mistake as to the facts in the case."

[1]His sons were soldiers in the war between the States.

Nat Turner's Sword.

the pine brush to reconnoitre, when Mr. Phipps suddenly spied him, leveled his gun, and demanded: "Who are you? Answer!" Nat immediately replied: "I am Nat Turner," and begged Phipps not to shoot. He knew the woods were full of armed men, and, if he succeeded in overcoming Phipps, he would only add one more crime to the list for which he must soon suffer. Not a gun had been fired for several weeks. This had been agreed upon as a signal of danger for the women and children to assemble at places of refuge.[1] Nat realized that the firing of the gun probably meant immediate death, and concluded it best to surrender and trust to fortune.[2]

Phipps now fired his gun in the air and the news of his capture spread so rapidly that in less than an hour one hundred men had collected at Mr. Edwards'. "Old Jeff" and Nelson had been sent to spread the news and assemble the people at the above place for a feast. Guns were fired on all sides and rendered the Sabbath one of general alarm and excitement. The women thought the firing meant that Nat had assembled another force and was laying waste the country. The approach of horsemen increased the alarm, and many females, hugging their infants to their bosoms, rushed to the swamps, misinterpreting the cry, "Nat is caught!" for "Nat is coming!" But alarm soon gave way to rejoicing. So great was public resentment at sight of the prisoner that it was difficult to convey him alive to Jerusalem. Persecuted with pin-pricks and soundly whipped, he was taken from Edwards' to Cross Keys, and thence from house to house, grinning and refusing to repent of his deeds. The negroes joined in the persecution and showed their contempt by

[1] The accidental firing of a gun at Jerusalem caused a general alarm, and the men rushed to arms, while the women and children assembled in churches for safety.
[2] Mr. Phipps was alone. Still he offered to give Nat a fair chance if he wished to fight. But, preferring unconditional surrender, Nat lay flat upon the ground and was firmly bound.

calling him "Old Nat," which is the title by which he is still known. Many citizens would scarcely know who was meant by the name Nat Turner.[1]

Sunday night Nat was taken to the home of Mr. David Westbrook, who was Phipps' nearest neighbor, and well guarded. It is said he was rolled downhill in a barrel. But many of the guard, being overcome with drink, the most conservative and reasonable citizens concealed the prisoner and protected him against excessive persecution. The next morning, Monday, October 31st, Nat was taken to Jerusalem, at which place he arrived at 1:15 p. m. The journey had necessarily been slow on account of the curiosity of the citizens and the necessity of securing him against insults and injury. He was well guarded, and reason and forbearance prevailed. The reports that he was burnt with hot irons, gashed with knives, and had coals of fire thrust into his mouth, at all of which Nat scoffed, are false. From the fact that he refused to repent of his deeds, he has been described as brave, and for this reason his persecution has been greatly exaggerated, ladies actually being accused of sticking pins in him. He could not have survived the persecutions which have been handed down by oral tradition, and his condition on his arrival at the jail disproved them. A citizen of Petersburg, who was in Jerusalem when Nat arrived, said that much praise was due the citizens of Southampton for their forbearance, and that not the least personal violence was offered him, who was the most miserable object he ever saw, dejected, emaciated, and ragged, possessed of no qualities of a hero or general, but without spirit, courage, and sagacity. Thus Nat was saved and his confession and treatment have

---

[1] "Aunt Viney," sister to Ben and Aaron, and Mrs. Musgrave's cook, asked to be allowed to whip him for causing her son's death. Her son had told Mrs. Musgrave of the rebellion of the negroes, but was later forced to join them. He escaped, however, but he had been seen with the insurgents, so was shot.

Home of Mr. Benjamin Phipps.

THE SOUTHAMPTON INSURRECTION. 95

vindicated the inhabitants of Southampton and proved that they were humane, considerate, and law-abiding people. He was delivered over to Justices James W. Parker and James Trezevant, who examined him for one and a half or two hours, Nat speaking intelligently, clearly, and without the least confusion, and advising other negroes not to attempt any such plots as he had undertaken through the misinterpretation of revelations. After the preliminary examination Nat was lodged in jail to await trial by the county court, great pains being taken to secure his safety by the appointment of a special guard.

This was the last capture. Much excitement and rashness had prevailed in the pursuit and capture of the rebels, but the cases of mercy and humanity overshadow those of barbarity and leave the decision in favor of the former. Other motives than humanity also worked in behalf of the culprits. In the first place, as many witnesses as possible were wanted in order to justify the people in the eyes of the world. Thus the four leaders—Hark, Nelson, Sam, and Nat—were spared and were instrumental in bringing many culprits to justice. Secondly, there was a very strong economic motive which was in favor of mercy. All slaves convicted by legal process and executed or transported, or who escaped before such trials, were paid for by the Commonwealth. But those who escaped before arrest or who were killed without trial were complete losses to the owners.[1] There were special reasons why Nat was spared. Public curiosity had been puzzled to understand the origin and purpose of this dreadful conspiracy and the motives which influenced its instigators. The insurgent slaves had all been destroyed or apprehended, tried and executed, with the exception of the leader and a few oth-

[1] Thus Richard Porter, Levi Waller, Peter Edwards and others petitioned for pay for slaves shot, but their claims were rejected by the Legislature of 1831.

ers, without revealing anything at all satisfactory in regard to these matters. Everything connected with the affair was wrapped in mystery. Thus the testimony of this fanatical leader was needed to clear away the cloud, which he did in his confession to Mr. Thomas R. Gray and the magisterial court. Further, Mr. Phipps was a poor man and had many friends. Consequently, he needed the rewards offered, which would not have been granted had the prisoners been mutilated or murdered.

TRIALS AND EXECUTIONS.—Fifty-three of the sixty or seventy negroes connected with the massacre were brought before the county court. The county jail was crowded with prisoners for days, and many had to be kept under guard on the outside for want of prison room. But no trial was begun before the eighth of September. Ample time was given for excitement and passion to give way to order and reason. Never were more pains taken to give fair trials and justice to prisoners. Howison's "History of Virginia" says: "The trials were conducted with a patience and care highly creditable to the magistracy of the county." Preliminary trials were given before two magistrates, and, if the prisoner was deemed guilty, he was sent on to the county court, but if innocent he was dismissed.

Free negroes could not be convicted by a county court. Of the five brought before the court four were sent on for further trial before the Superior Circuit Court, the evidence being sufficient, and one was acquitted. The county court was composed of all the magistrates of the county, of whom five were necessary for a quorum. A unanimous vote of the magistrates present at a trial was required for conviction. The Court of Oyer and Terminer, which convicted Nat Turner and his comrades, was composed of the most distinguished and intelligent men of the county, some of whom had been members of the famous convention of 1829. No one was allowed to

Cross Keys.
(Showing the Old Store House in Which Some of the Insurgents Were Imprisoned.)

THE SOUTHAMPTON INSURRECTION.   97

preside as a justice who was interested in, or prejudiced against, the prisoners. Nor were witnesses permitted who were known to be biased. A separate trial was assigned each prisoner and every possible chance given him to summon witnesses and defend himself. Also, the three most prominent and able lawyers available—W. C. Parker, James R. French, and Thomas R. Gray—were assigned as counsel. They exerted every possible effort to secure justice and protection for the prisoners. Several were acquitted on the testimony of their owners as to their good characters. Trial was postponed if further witnesses were needed, and several prisoners were discharged on the ground of insufficient evidence. Invariably the negroes pleaded not guilty of the charge brought forth in the arraignment of the able prosecuting attorney, Merewether B. Brodnax. On the 6th of September, as it had been intimated that the militia would soon be discharged, the court, which had been in continual session since a week succeeding the first arrest, unanimously petitioned General Eppes to retain fifty men as a necessary guard to the prisoners. The young negroes, too, and those deceived or forced into the insurrection had their sentences commuted from execution to transportation, upon the recommendation of the justices, of the attorney for the Commonwealth, and of their counsel. These are evidence that the court was uninfluenced by motives of personal safety or prejudices against the prisoners.[1]

All the negroes known to have been connected with the plot were executed or transported before the 1st of Octo-

[1] Three boys, Nathan, Tom, and Davy, belonging to Mr. Nat Francis, were forced to participate, and threatened with their lives if they escaped. The oldest of these was only fifteen years old and, besides, was deformed. They were assigned one of the above-mentioned lawyers as counsel, tried and condemned to be hung, but on the recommendation of the court they were transported.

ber, except Nat and one other.[1] It was very important that the trial of the leader should be conducted with especial fairness and patience. The court met on Saturday, November 5th, ten of the leading men of the county,[2] instead of the customary five, presided as justices, and ordered the summoning of a sufficient additional guard to repel any attempt that might be made to take the prisoners from the custody of the sheriff. After assigning William C. Parker counsel for the defense, the court proceeded to the consideration of the bill of information filed against the prisoner by Mr. Brodnax, attorney for the Commonwealth. Nat, upon his arraignment, pleaded not guilty, declaring to his counsel that he did not feel so.

The first witness sworn was Levi Waller, who stated that he saw the prisoner, whom he knew before, at his home, and saw him force several reluctant slaves to mount their horses and follow him. He further stated that Nat was in command of the forces. Mr. James Trezevant stated that he and Mr. James Parker were the justices before whom the prisoners were examined previous to his commitment; that the prisoner was at the time in confinement, but no threats or promises were held out to

[1] Of this number only one was a woman, she being the only female in any way guilty of participation, with the exception of Charlotte, who threatened the life of Mr. Lavinia Francis. This woman was Lucy, the slave of Mr. John T. Barrow, who attempted to prevent the escape of Mrs. Barrow, and who was convicted on the evidence of her mistress and other important witnesses, among these Dr. Robert T. Musgrave. On the 26th of September she was taken from the jail, and, riding upon her coffin, to the place of execution, and was hung and buried in the well-known burying ground of the insurgents.

[2] Jeremiah Cobb, Samuel B. Hines, James D. Massenburg, James W. Parker, Robert Goodwin, James Trezevant, Oris Browne, Carr Bowers, Thomas Pretlow, and Richard A. Urquhart. Mr. Cobb presided over the court as chief magistrate and delivered the sentence, which has been deemed worthy of "a United States Chief Justice of today."

Home of Mr. James Trezevant (Magistrate).

him to make any disclosure; that he admitted that he was
one of the insurgents engaged in the late insurrection and
the chief among them, that he gave to his master and mistress—Mr. Travis and his wife—the first blow before they
were dispatched, that he killed Miss Peggy Whitehead,
that he was with the insurgents from their first movement
to their dispersion on the Tuesday morning after the insurrection took place; that he gave a long account of the
motives that led him finally to commence the bloody scene
which took place; that he pretended to have had signs
and omens from God that he should embark in the desperate attempt; that his comrades and even he were
impressed with the belief that he could, by the imposition
of his hands, cure diseases; that he related a particular
instance in which it was believed that he had in that
manner effected a cure upon one of his comrades; and
that he went on to detail a medley of incoherent, confused
opinions about his connection with God, his command
over the clouds, etc., etc., which he had been entertaining
as far back as 1826. Other witnesses were examined and
Mr. W. C. Parker exerted his best efforts in behalf of his
client. He had made a thorough examination of the incidents of the massacre, and was well acquainted with it
from beginning to end. He had defended at least one-third
of the prisoners brought before the court, among them
Hark, a most intelligent and enthusiastic conspirator, who
had been introduced as witness in many trials and had testified to the innocence or guilt of the prisoners. But the
testimony was so strong against Nat that the case was
submitted without argument. Nat could not plead cruelty at the hands of an imperious and barbarous master
as an excuse for the crime, for he confessed that he had
had a kind and considerate master, and, in fact, an overindulgent one. Nor could the plea of insanity be made, for
the prisoner had answered questions most intelligently,

100   THE SOUTHAMPTON INSURRECTION.

and showed a marked degree of sound judgment. Consequently, the court was of the opinion that the prisoner was guilty in manner and form as in the information against him alleged. It was then demanded of him if he had or knew anything to say why the court should not proceed to judgment and execution against him of and upon the premises. Nat replied that he had made a full confession to Mr. Thomas R. Gray.[1] Having nothing to say in his defense, he was commanded to stand up and attend to the sentence of the court, which was pronounced by Jeremiah Cobb.[2]

---

[1] The confession was made on Tuesday, the 1st of November, and two succeeding days thereafter in the county jail. Mr. Gray thoroughly examined him and compared the testimony of each day's interview with that of the preceding day or days and with the confessions of all the prisoners who had been previously tried and whom Nat had neither seen nor had any knowledge of since the 22d of August. Mr. Gray, too, had taken an active part in defending these prisoners. But Nat proved accurate and did not blunder.

[2] The sentence was in the following words: "You have been arraigned and tried before the court and convicted of one of the highest crimes in our criminal code. You have been convicted of plotting, in cold blood, the indiscriminate destruction of men, of helpless women, and of infant children. The evidence before us leaves not a shadow of doubt but that your hands were often imbued in the blood of the innocent; and your own confession tells us that they were stained with the blood of a master, in your own language, 'too indulgent.' Could I stop here, your crime would be sufficiently aggravated; but the original contriver of a plan deep and deadly, one that can never be effected, you managed so far to put into execution as to deprive us of many of our most valuable citizens; and this was done when they were asleep and defenseless, under circumstances shocking to humanity. And while upon this part of the subject, I cannot but call attention to the poor, misguided wretches who have gone before you. They are not a few in number—they were your bosom associates—and the blood of all cries out aloud and calls upon you as the author of their misfortune. Yes! You forced them unprepared from time to eternity. Borne down by the load of guilt, your only justification is that you were borne away by fanaticism. If this be true, from my soul I pity you; and while you have my sympathies, I am, nevertheless, called upon to pass the sentence of the court. The time between this and your execution will

Southampton Court House.

THE SOUTHAMPTON INSURRECTION. 101

The sentence was received, as his late deeds and intentions had been spoken of, with calm, deliberate composure. Mr. Gray says: "The expression of his fiendlike face when excited by enthusiasm, still bearing the stains of helpless innocence about him, clothed with rags and covered with chains, yet daring to raise his manacled hands to heaven, with a spirit soaring above the attributes of man, I looked on him and my blood curdled in my veins." Without an exception the insurgent slaves apprehended, tried and convicted, had, under no coercion or persuasion, confessed the names of all connected with the conspiracy, the part they took, the names of those killed, etc., but they pleaded that they were forced or misled by the leaders. They could not tell what they expected to accomplish, but invariably referred to the confidence and belief the leader had inspired in them. They were thus ignorant of their undertaking, had no other purpose than plunder and murder, and now tried to exculpate themselves. But Nat Turner explained the entire plot, and frankly acknowledged his full participation in the guilt of the transaction, and that he was not only the contriver, but struck the first blow toward the execution of the conspiracy.

On the 11th of November the last sentence of the court was executed. Nat Turner and three of his associates were hanged, one having been sentenced before his arrest, and the others convicted upon his testimony. Fifty-three negroes had been arraigned. Of these seventeen were executed and twelve transported. The rest were discharged, except the four free negroes sent on to the Superior Court. Three of the four were executed. The bodies

necessarily be short, and your only hope must be in another world. The judgment of the court is, that you be taken hence to the jail from whence you came, thence to the place of execution, and on Friday next, between the hours of 10 a. m. and 2 p. m., be hung by the neck until you are dead! dead! dead! and may the Lord have mercy upon your soul."

102 THE SOUTHAMPTON INSURRECTION.

of those executed, with one exception, were buried in a decent and becoming manner. That of Nat Turner was delivered to the doctors, who skinned it and made grease of the flesh.[1] His skeleton was for many years in the possession of Dr. Massenberg, but has since been misplaced.[2]

[1] The famous remedy of the doctors of ante-bellum days—castor oil—was long dreaded for fear it was "old Nat's" grease, and it is doubtful if the old prejudice has entirely died out among the older darkies.

[2] There are many citizens still living who have seen Nat's skull. It was very peculiarly shaped, resembling the head of a sheep, and at least three-quarters of an inch thick. Mr. R. S. Barham's father owned a money purse made of his hide. During the French Revolution, books are said to have been bound in the skins of victims of the guillotine, and now in the British Museum books are exhibited bound in tanned human skin. Our newspapers have recorded frequently that in other States are preserved many memorials of like morbid and depraved taste.

Southampton Jail.

Mr. Collin Kitchen.
(Born September 12, 1806. He was One of the Special Police Appointed to Guard the Jail).

CHAPTER III.

RELATIONS TO SLAVERY AND THE SOUTH.

CONDITION OF THE NEGROES.—Southampton is one of the most prosperous counties of Virginia. It is the dividing line between the agricultural systems of the Southern and Middle Atlantic States, growing the products of both sections to perfection, and requiring a diversity of agricultural knowledge seldom found elsewhere. Vegetables grow in abundance and variety, and the distance from a market has alone hindered their cultivation to a greater extent. The soil is especially suited to the cultivation of grain, and thus the farmers are independent, the extensive low-grounds furnishing acorns in abundance for the droves of hogs annually slaughtered. The county is the banner cotton section of the State, and its average production per acre is as great as that of any of the older cotton States. This is a fact seldom noticed, Virginia not being especially adapted to the production of cotton. Her peanuts are superior to those of any country. Tobacco is also one of the money crops, and apples, pears, peaches, and other fruits grow luxuriantly and yield abundantly. Some of the largest and finest apple orchards of the State are found here, and in former years— not so much so now—these orchards received much attention and great care. They yielded large quantities of apples, which were manufactured into the finest brandy and cider vinegar known in the trade.[1] Southampton apple brandy, as well as Southampton bacon, has for years been the best in the market, and a citizen is strongly

---

[1] It is within the memory of the youngest citizens that these distilleries have generally disappeared.

impressed with this fact by the gentle reminders of those whom he tells of his native county. Every farm has its apple orchard, and many an old settlement is today known only by the decaying apple trees which mark the spot. Apple brandy was the principal source of revenue. Cotton, corn, and tobacco grew in the orchard, and while they were maturing the apples were gathered and manufactured into brandy and cider. Thus the apple crop was clear profit. The following are the words of a native of Southampton at the time of our narrative: "Apple brandy was a factor, and an important one, in those bloody scenes. But for that many more would have been murdered. Nearly everybody at that time had an orchard, and it was probably the largest source of revenue in a county where revenues were small. I know my father's income was derived chiefly from the brandy he made and sold. Whenever they (the negroes) stopped in their raids they drank abundantly of it."[1]

It is true that the revenues were small at this time, and likewise that all supplies were produced at home—nails, horseshoes, and plows, as well as vehicles. Every farm had its carpenter and shoemaker, who was, in many cases, the master, and the weaving house was, until recently, to be seen in the rear of the dwelling, presided over by the mistress and her chief colored weaver. The old slaves also made the best physicians and nurses. They were gentle and sympathetic, and their services were especially valued. The gradual disappearance of this class of negroes marks the changes of modern times. Bishop Potter, of New York, says: "I listened the other day to the story of a charming woman, of marked culture and

[1] This is evidently one cause why more discipline was not observed and more whites not killed by Nat Turner and his band. Every person who witnessed the scenes of 1831, men and women, even the most earnest advocates of temperance, concludes his or her story with the honest confession, "This is one case in which brandy did good."

refinement, as she depicted, with unconscious grace and art, the life of a gentlewoman of her own age and class— she was young and fair and keenly sympathetic—on a Southern plantation before the Civil War. One got such a new impression of those whom, under other skies and in large ignorance of their personal ministries or sacrifices, we have been wont to picture as indolent, exclusive, indifferent to the sorrow and disease and ignorance that, on a great rice or cotton or sugar plantation in the old days, were all about them; and one learned, with a new sense of reverence for all that is best in womanhood, how, in days that are now gone forever, there were under such conditions the most skillful beneficence and the most untiring sympathies. But, in the times of which I speak, the service on the plantation for the sick slave (which, an ungracious criticism might have suggested, since a slave was ordinarily a valuable piece of property, had something of a sordid element in it) was matched in communities and under conditions where no such suspicion was possible. No one who knows anything of life in our smaller communities at the beginning of the century can be ignorant of what I mean. There was no village or smallest aggregation of families that had not its Abigail, its 'Aunt Hannah,' its 'Uncle Ben,' who, when there was sickness or want or sorrow in a neighbor's house, was always on hand to sympathize and to succor."[1]

The slaves were acquainted with the diseases of hogs, cattle, and all domestic animals. In fact, the best veterinarians of ante-bellum days were slaves, and much of the modern science is indebted to them. Every farm had its negro chaplain (negro preacher), who was only second to the master, the spiritual adviser of all. The Richmond Times of October 26, 1899, says:

"A few months ago an old negro down South was

[1] Popular Science Monthly, October, 1899.

arraigned in court on the charge of criminal assault. He had no evidence to offer in support of his innocence, except his previously good character. He introduced the white men of the community to the court and called upon them to give evidence as to his standing. They all cheerfully stood up and told the court, under oath, that, so far as they knew to the contrary, he had led an exemplary life. The Commonwealth's attorney refused to prosecute. The case was dismissed, and the judge, from the bench, complimented the old man on the high character that he had proved. 'Yes,' said the old man, through his tears, 'and I got that character from my old marster, who showed me the right way.'" The more intelligent negroes also acted as advocates before the tribunal presided over by the master.

Consequently there was a division of labor under the slave regime exceeding that of any farm of the present day, which made it possible to assign each set of hands their duty and to dispense with the cruelties which have been mistakenly attributed to the slave system employed in the production of large tobacco and cotton crops. There were valuable cotton and tobacco farms, but none of them were very extensive, and no one owned more than seventy-five or eighty slaves, the average number owned by a family being five or six. No overseer was needed, and when employed he occupied the position of general director and not of arbitrary lord and master. He was responsible to the owner of the slaves, but the negro foreman also exercised authority and reported irregularities to his master. Thus the former was restrained by fear of losing his position. But the general custom was for each master to manage for himself, and place a foreman in the person of one of their own number over each squad of slaves assigned to a special duty. This system dispensed more or less with that class of "poor whites" which has so often been depicted as the evil of slavery.

THE SOUTHAMPTON INSURRECTION.

They did not consider it a disgrace to work side by side with the slaves, since they did not have the legal equality of the negro continually thrust at them.

With the consciousness of being able to rise to the position of foreman, each slave was incited to interest in his work. He realized that his master's interest was his. The hog feeder was proud to exhibit his drove of hogs, the herdsman and shepherd pointed to their flocks with pride, and the hostler boasted of the fastest and best bred horses on the road. The old "stiller" smiled when his brandy was praised, and the cook was aware of her superiority. The old nurse was conscious of her power and the love and respect of all the whites. Each department had its negro foreman and his or her associates, the former a master in his profession, instructing the latter in the mysteries thereof. By means of this class system among the slaves, the barriers of which could be overcome by diligence and respect, they were controlled with ease and inspired with ambition far surpassing that of the negro of today, who is conscious of his inability to attain the boasted equality with whites, and consequently meditates revenge and cherishes hatred.

Fealty and diligence were also encouraged by confidence on the part of the master, who rewarded his servants with crops, gardens, and other property, the proceeds from which were spent at their discretion. Slaves were often allowed to choose their own employer and make their own contracts.[1] Holidays were frequent. From sunrise to sunset was the time for labor, but breakfast and dinner, in the meantime, occupied at least three hours. This limit was not strictly insisted on, as is shown by the reply of an old negro, who, when asked by his mistress why he was sitting on the fence while the sun was still above the horizon, replied: "Waitin' for de sun to

[1] Journals of Virginia Legislature: Page, Social Life in Virginia.

108   THE SOUTHAMPTON INSURRECTION.

go down, mum." Saturday was a holiday for the deserving, and Sunday was spent as the slave liked. If he was not promptly on hand Monday morning he was not punished.[1]

The emancipation sentiment in Southampton was very strong, and it was fostered by the numerous Quakers of the county. In the county records are to be found numbers of emancipation deeds. Thus the slaves were encouraged by the possibility of freedom. The free negroes were prosperous and many owned land and were employed by the whites as any other laborers. They were also assisted in their efforts, if they wished, to emigrate to Liberia.[2] They increased rapidly, and from a proportion of less than one to ten in 1790 the ratio of free negroes to slaves had decreased to an average of one to every four and a third in 1830.[3] The county had a greater proportion of free negroes than any of the neighboring counties except Nansemond and Isle of Wight. The whites had, in the meantime, remained about the same,

[1] An old negro who knew Nat Turner said the latter could go away on Sunday, and if he did not return until Monday morning nothing was said to him. This, he continued, was the case with all the faithful slaves before the insurrection, but afterward if one did not return in time, "dis here thing was tuck off, an' de back picked jest like a chicken pickin' corn."

[2] Hon. Anthony W. Gardner, born January 24, 1824, of free parents, in Southampton county, emigrated with them to Liberia in January, 1831, and in 1879 was elected president of the colony. His inaugural address was eloquent and able, and he rendered valuable service to his country.—Sixty-second Report of the American Colonization Society.

[3] Table showing the population of Southampton for each decade from 1790 to 1830:

Year.	Whites.	All other free persons.	Slaves.	Total.
1790	6,312	559	5,993	12,864
1800	6,461	839	6,625	13,925
1810	5,982	1,109	6,406	13,497
1820	6,127	1,306	6,737	14,170
1830	6,573	1,745	7,756	16,074

THE SOUTHAMPTON INSURRECTION. 109

while the free blacks increased on an average of thirty and the slaves on one of forty-four per year during the forty years from 1790 to 1830.[1]

The slaves were cared for with the greatest kindness.[2] The white master did not treat his slave as his ox. Slavery was simply domestic servitude, under practically efficient guarantees against ill-treatment. The system was more on the order of that in the Mosaic law, where the slave was a member of the family, and to insult or maltreat a slave was an insult which had to be atoned for upon the field of honor. The slave quarters formed a long street in the rear of the dwelling of the master, resembling a mediaeval village community, and during the cold winter nights the last duty of the master before retiring was to visit these quarters to see that the children were well provided with food, covering, and fuel. In many respects the slave fared better than the master.[3] There was an

[1] Table showing population of counties contiguous to Southampton:

County.	Whites.	Slaves.	Free blacks
Greenesville	2,104	4,681	332
Isle of Wight	7,023	4,272	1,222
Nansemond	5,143	4,943	1,698
Surry	2,865	3,377	866
Sussex	4,118	7,736	866

The populations of the neighboring counties of North Carolina were as follows: Bertie, 12,276; Gates, 7,866; Hertford, 8,541; Northampton, 13,103, of whom about one-half were blacks, and a large proportion of the latter were free.

[2] It was from this direction that the evil came, and not from bad treatment, and the South now thanks the God of Battle for the freedom of the slaves.

[3] They had no responsibility and never suffered for food or clothing. The general consensus of opinion among the old slaves is that they fared better as slaves than at the present time. This want of responsibility explains the more rapid increase of the negroes as slaves than as free citizens. This also accounts for the fact that pulmonary diseases were almost unheard of among the slaves. The want of such care at the present day in turn explains the great prevalence of the disease, among the negroes of the present day.

110 THE SOUTHAMPTON INSURRECTION.

attachment between the blacks and whites which is difficult to describe, and which was exhibited until within a few years past, when the population of Southampton was contaminated by the influx of foreigners employed in sawmills and railroad work.[1] Both races were benefited and a noble people developed, the native blacks being the equals of any of their race.[2] Gentle treatment rendered the slave not only more faithful and affectionate, but more intelligent, and his condition, in fact, approximated that of a free servant. Slaves were the happiest laboring class in the world, and under these most favorable conditions furnished a contradiction of the "orthodox" economic theory as to the unproductiveness of slave labor.[3] The oldest inhabitants of the county state that Southampton saw its most prosperous and progressive days between 1830 and 1861, notwithstanding the fact that tobacco and cotton had declined, and the most severe

[1] This spirit was not even lessened by the horrors of the Nat Turner insurrection. Gilbert, who belonged to Major Thomas Pretlow, one of the justices who sat on the trial of Nat, was given the privilege of being free by Mrs. Pretlow, but he declared he would never leave the family, and died a member of it. During the war Federal forces visited the neighboring counties, but very few of the negroes of Southampton ran away, and those who escaped did so through the persuasion of the scouts roaming the country.

[2] The superiority and more refined feelings of the negro of Southampton and the foreign influences are illustrated by the following. One of them expressed his horror and disgust at the terrible butchery committed by Nat and his band at Mr. Waller's, and said it was an outrage. A negro who was on a visit to the county for the purpose of learning more about the insurrection was incensed at this remark and replied that it was the desert of the whites and that the insurrection was not cruel enough. This incident occurred only a few years ago.

[3] It did away with idleness and improved not only the condition of the people in general, but the products of labor were greater. For instance, the hog and chicken cholera, now so prevalent in the county, were comparatively unknown. Their prevalence now, no doubt, is due to the half-fed dogs, hogs, etc., which roam the country and which then did not exist.

THE SOUTHAMPTON INSURRECTION. 111

panic in the history of the United States occurred in 1837 and 1841.[1] The condition of the Southern States is much improved since 1865. This is partly the effect of the general advance of civilization, and cannot be entirely attributed to the abolition of slavery. Besides, the greatest advance is seen in the cities, while in the rural districts, where the greatest number of slaves were owned, the condition of agriculture is very little improved, and in some sections is on a decline. The system of labor seems to have been an ideal one.

Previous to 1831 there had been only three negroes executed and four transported for crimes in Southampton, and the neighboring counties had equally as good records. Isle of Wight had one executed; Nansemond transported one and executed three before and executed one for conspiracy and rebellion in 1831, though thirty or forty were tried; Surry executed one and transported one before and transported one in that year for participation in the Southampton insurrection; Sussex had one executed and three transported before, and four executed and two transported in 1831 for suspicious connection with the same plot; Greenesville had none executed and none transported before or during 1831. The only case of discontent among the slaves on record in Southampton previous to the Nat Turner insurrection was in October, 1799, and that was participated in by only four negroes, who had been smuggled from Maryland. There had been suspicions of rebellions in other sections, but the fidelity of the slaves here had never been doubted. Nat had acted fanatically and Nelson Williams had actually said that there was going to be trouble, but no one could conceive

---

[1] "Tobacco has fallen beyond all calculation. Cotton is down from seventeen to ten cents per pound. Instead of exporting any breadstuffs, we have been compelled by the scarcity of our harvests to draw upon the granaries of Europe."—Richmond Enquirer (Niles, L.II, p. 131).

of the disloyalty of the negroes. A citizen of the county, living near Jerusalem at the time of the insurrection, says: "Southampton is a pretty large county. Whether there were premonitions of coming events in the neighborhood of Cross Keys, where the movement occurred, I know not. I think it came upon the people suddenly and without warning. In our section of the county nothing ever happened to forecast such an event. We had no reason to suspect the loyalty of the negroes. I recollect that Capt. Billy Kitchen, one of our neighbors, had quite a number of slaves. One of his slaves had for a wife our cook. On hearing of the insurrection, he took his family into a piece of woodland, cut down trees, erected barriers, something in the shape of fortifications, armed his slaves with axes, hoes, pikes, and anything at hand, and, having full faith in their loyalty and devotion, he left to join the main body in pursuit of the revolutionists."[1] The words of Mr. Gray well described the condition of the county at the time, the nature of the plot, and its murderous execution: "It will thus," he says, "appear that whilst upon the surface society wore a calm and peaceful aspect; whilst not one note of preparation was heard to warn the devoted inhabitants of woe and death, a gloomy fanatic was revolving in the recesses of his own dark, bewildered, and overwrought mind schemes of indiscriminate massacre of the whites—schemes too fearfully executed as far as his fiendish band proceeded in their desolating march. No cry for mercy penetrated their flinty bosoms. No acts

---

[1]Such cases of confidence were shown on all sides. Mr. John Ivey, who lived near Haley's Bridge, about ten miles from Cross Keys, left his plantation in charge of his slaves. One of the negroes caught a horse and started to join the insurgents. But the other slaves caught him and delivered him to their leader, "old John," who gave him a thorough thrashing and chained him until his master returned. This was the case, though Mr. Ivey told John that he might have all the farm and property if he did not return.

of remembered kindness made the least impression upon the remorseless murderers. Men, women, and children, from hoary age to helpless infancy, were involved in the same cruel fate. Never did a band of savages do their work of death more unsparingly. Apprehension of their own personal safety seems to have been the only principle of restraint in the whole course of their bloody proceedings."

CAUSES OF THE INSURRECTION.—Such was the state of society in which was reared Nat Turner. He was endowed with a natural intelligence and quickness possessed by few men, with a mind capable of high attainments, but warped and perverted by the influence of early as well as later impressions. His case should be an important and useful lesson in the experience of a mind like his endeavoring to grapple with things beyond its reach. He was a careful student of the Bible, a Baptist preacher, read the newspapers and every book within his reach, and listened attentively to the discussions of political and social questions by the best and most enlightened men of the country. His sphere of action was too small for such a mind, and, consequently, he deemed it possible to conquer the county, march to the Dismal Swamp, collecting the slaves as he went, and so gradually overcome the State, as the Americans had the British in the Revolutionary War, all to "call the attention of the civilized world to the condition of his race." After his failure he confessed that he had been mistaken in the practicability of his scheme, frustrated both by the ready assembling of the whites and the want of discipline among his men.

Cruel treatment was not a motive for the rebellion. If this had been the case, it would have been urged in mitigation of Nat's punishment. On the contrary, he stated in his testimony that he had no reason to complain of Mr. Travis, who was a kind master, and placed the greatest confidence in him.[1] Nat was a complete fanatic, and believed the Lord had destined him to free his race. The red tint of the autumn leaves was a sign of the blood which was to be shed.[2] And his last text at Barnes' Church, a few days before the massacre, indicates the trend of his mind. It reads: "And I saw, and behold a white horse: and he that sat on him had a bow; and a crown was given unto him: and he went forth conquering and to conquer."[3] Though Nat was a religious fanatic, yet he deemed any means justifiable for the accomplishment of his purpose and for making the impression that he was a prophet a. ˙ servant of God. He wrote hieroglyphics and quotations on leaves and blades of fodder, and these found, according to his prediction, caused the slaves to believe him a miraculous being, endowed with supernatural powers. He spat blood at pleasure, but it proved to be the coloring matter of the log-wood, stolen from his master's dye pots. At his baptism crowds gathered, some from curiosity and others from a belief in his prophecy that a white dove would descend from heaven and alight upon his shoulder. This prophecy explains the reviling to which he refers in his confession, no doubt, with the intention of making the impression that the white people disapproved of religious toleration. That Nat was believed must not be taken as proof of the ignorance and exclusive superstition of the blacks. It is the custom to consider the whites as far advanced as they are at present, and the slaves as debased, ignorant, and superstitious creatures as in their native state. But the eclipse of the sun in February, and its peculiar appearance in

---

[1] He told Mrs. Musgrave, who had been confined to her bed on account of the great excitement, that to kill his master's family was the most difficult task he ever had to perform.

[2] He told Mrs. Francis, the mother of Mrs. Travis, and Mr. Salathiel Francis, that he killed her children because the Lord had commanded him.

[3] Revelations, vi, 2.

Tree Under Which Nat Turner Was Hung.

Tree Marking the Place of Burial of Insurgent Negroes, Standing near the Tree under which they were Hung.

August, 1831, had as grave an effect upon the former as upon the latter. The "green" or "blue" day is still remembered by some of our citizens, and at the time something terrible was hourly expected.[1] Upon the scaffold Nat declared that after his execution it would grow dark and rain for the last time. It did actually rain, and there was for some time a dry spell. This alarmed many of the whites as well as the negroes. Conjuring was the Southern counterpart of the old Puritan belief in witchcraft. It is generally attributed to the negroes, some of whom professed to be "conjur doctors,"[2] but many a gouty master believed himself conjured. Nor are such signs of superstition and fear wanting at the present day. The negroes are still afraid to pass graveyards and places where murders have been committed, and see the wrath of God in every unusual occurrence.

Thus the insurrection "was not instigated by motives of revenge or sudden anger, but the result of long deliberation and a settled purpose of mind, the offspring of gloomy fanaticism acting upon materials but too well prepared for such impressions," and of love of self-importance, encouraged by the efforts of negro preachers, who were influenced by external affairs, and employed in circulating inflammatory and seditious periodicals.[3] Those

[1] Judith, Marion Harland, p. 61 et seq.; Forest, "Norfolk and Vicinity," pp. 192-193.

[2] Some of these abuse the confidence imposed in them and frighten some of their weaker brethren by threats and great pretensions.

[3] The Norfolk Herald, of August 29, 1831: "We have just received letters from Winton and Murfreesboro, N. C. * * * Our Winton friend says: * * * 'It seems that the whole affair was arranged by negro preachers who were suffered to hold their meetings at pleasure, by day and by night, and it seems those scoundrels have poisoned the minds of the negroes.'" The negro who was taken for Nat in Botetourt county was a negro preacher, as was also the negro condemned in Nansemond county for signifying his intention to join a conspiracy against the whites at the solicitation of a negro preacher from Isle of Wight.

who have received most are the most jealous and ready to complain. Nat Turner, as the Southampton slaves in general, was like a spoiled child, who, having been allowed too many privileges in youth, soon thinks he ought to be master of all he surveys. The calling of a Constitutional Convention, to meet in October, 1829, inspired in the slaves of Matthews, Isle of Wight, and the neighboring counties hopes of emancipation, and in case of failure of such declaration a determination to rebel and massacre the whites. Doubtless Nat had heard the same subjects discussed, and, being conscious of the results of the convention, which not only failed to emancipate the slaves, but limited the right of suffrage to the whites, he considered it time to carry out his threats.[1] He was undoubtedly inspired with the hope of freedom, and the mere discussion of emancipation by a convention may have led him to believe that many of the whites would sympathize with his schemes. He is said to have passed the home of some poor white people because he considered it useless to kill those who thought no better of themselves than they did of the negroes. He also said that after he had gained a firm foothold he intended to spare all the women and children and the men who offered no resistance. But the watchword of all was indiscriminate slaughter and plunder.

Nat was certainly no coward, and would never have surrendered to Phipps, except that he saw no chance of escape, and thus believed it better to surrender and trust to fortune. Hark was also brave, but not one of the others could claim this quality or that of religious fanat-

[1] In a pamphlet published in 1830 by a negro of Boston this convention is spoken of. The author refers to the "Great, happy, and eloquent harangues" of John Randolph, in which he claims Ohio as a slave State, and accuses the "Honorable Slaveholder" o:' deceiving the ignorant.—Walker's Appeal, p. 77.

THE SOUTHAMPTON INSURRECTION. 117

icism.[1] Nat, when he was asked what he had done with all the money taken, said he had received only four and six pence (75 cents), and, turning to a free negro, who was also a prisoner, declared, "You know money was not my object." Still, each negro meditated returning within a few days to take possession of his master's home.[2] Thus the houses and barns were not burned, nor the furniture damaged, except so far as to enable them to procure the valuables therein, though victims were robbed of their clothes, jewelry, and other valuables.

Some say that victims were murdered and no further outrages committed, and the fact has been attributed to "the very success of their hideous enterprise,"[3] but this is an error.[4] Women were insulted, and it is said that Nat offered protection to one beautiful girl if she would consent to be his wife, but death was to this noble woman a blessing in comparison with such a prospect. Bodies were chopped to pieces and tortured to death, and chil-

[1]The Richmond Enquirer, of August 26, 1831, says: "It is supposed most of these marauders and murderers were runaway negroes, who had broken in on the whites for robbing and other mischief. There is no appearance of concert among the slaves, nothing that can deserve the name of insurrection, which it was originally denominated."

[2]Some actually did this. Mr. Collin Kitchen, when he returned home after the insurrection had been suppressed, found one of his servants dressed in his wife's clothes, entertaining one of her friends. She had taken possession of the farm and was eating at his table and sleeping in his bed.

[3]Howison's History of Virginia.

[4]Governor Floyd, in his message calling the attention of the Legislature of 1831-32 to the necessity of immediate legislation on the subject of slavery, said: "Whilst we were enjoying the abundance of last season, rejoicing in the peace and quiet of domestic comfort and safety, we were suddenly aroused from that serenity by receiving information that a portion of our fellow-citizens had fallen victims to the relentless fury of assassins and murderers, even whilst wrapped in profound sleep, and that these deeds had been perpetrated in a spirit of cruelty unknown to savage warfare, even in their most revolting form."

dren had their brains knocked out.[1] The Enquirer of August 30th, says: "What strikes us as the most remarkable thing in this matter is the horrible ferocity of those monsters. They remind one of a parcel of blood-thirsty wolves making down from the Alps, or, rather, like a former incursion of the Indians upon the white settlements."[2] All along the route lay the murdered victims, so mangled by the murderers and disfigured by hogs as to be unrecognizable even to their friends. Nor did those negroes escape who refused to participate in the massacre. One of the slaves of Mr. Nat Francis, who was milking when the insurgents arrived, had his heel-strings cut because he refused to join them. Such were the horrors and depredations that they have been handed down to our own time. As wrote a citizen of 1831, "Many a mother, as she presses her infant darling to her bosom, will shudder at the recollection of Nat Turner and his ferocious band of miscreants."

The influence of the French refugees still lingers in some of the customs and habits of the people of Baltimore, Norfolk, Charleston, and New Orleans, and for years after the San Domingo rebellion negroes were heard to refer to those scenes. No foreign event ever created a greater impression on the Southern portion of the United States,

[1] A writer to the Beacon says: "That part of the county which we have passed through is comparatively deserted. We saw several children whose brains were knocked out, and have accounts of the murder of sixty-eight men, women and children. Several reported to have been killed were found hid in the woods, but more than fifty-five, as commonly believed, were killed."

[2] The Norfolk Herald, of August 26, contains the following: "Indeed, nothing is known with certainty, but the painful fact that fifty-eight persons have been massacred. All accounts, however, concur in representing the affair as one which originated with a few without any concert, or understanding, even, with the slaves of their own county. * * * The number that commenced the bloody work was only seven—three white men and four blacks—mere marauders bent on plunder; but having steeped their hands in human sacrifice became infuriated and like bloodhounds pursued their game of murder in mere wanton sport."

contiguous to whose shores lay this island, calling attention to the fact that such a catastrophe was possible in the United States so soon as the slaves increased in the same proportion.[1] This fact had much influence upon

[1] But the influence of the French Revolution and, through it, of the San Domingo rebellion, was realized before such an increase of the slave population. The negroes of Louisiana rose in rebellion, and but for disagreement among themselves would have murdered many of the inhabitants of this province. Mr. Charles Guarre, who was later elected to a seat in the United States Senate but resigned, in his "Essai Historique sur la Louisiane," says: "The white population of Louisiana was not the only population which was agitated by the French Revolution. The blacks, encouraged without doubt with the success their race had obtained in San Domingo, dreamed of liberty and sought to shake off the yoke. The insurrection was planned at Pointe Coupee, which was then an isolated parish and in which the number of slaves was considerable. The conspiracy took birth on the plantation of Mr. Julien Poydras, a rich planter, who was then traveling in the United States, and spread rapidly through the parish. The death of all the whites was resolved. Happily, the conspirators could not agree upon the day for the massacre, and from this disagreement resulted a quarrel, which led to the discovery of the plot. The militia of the parish immediately took arms, and the Baron de Carondelet caused them to be supported by the troops of the line. It was resolved to arrest and punish the principal conspirators. The slaves opposed it; but they were quickly dispersed, with the loss of twenty of their number killed on the spot. Fifty of the insurgents were condemned to death, sixteen were executed in different parts of the parish; the rest were put on board a galley and hung at intervals all along the river as far as New Orleans (a distance of one hundred and fifty miles). The severity of the chastisement intimidated the blacks, and all retired to perfect order." Mr. Benton said in the United States Senate in 1835 that the effect of the Society in Paris—"Les Amis des Noirs"--upon the French island was known to the world, "but what is not known to the world, or not sufficiently known to it, is that the same societies which wrapped in flame and drenched in blood the beautiful island, which was then a garden and is now a wilderness, were the means of exciting an insurrection on our continent—in Louisiana, where a French slave population existed and where the language of Les Amis des Noirs could be understood, and where their emissaries could go. The knowledge of this event ought to be better known, both to show the dangers of these societies, however distant, and though oceans may roll between them and their victims, and the fate of the slaves who may be excited to insurrection by them on any part of the American Continent."—Thirty Years in the United States Senate, vol. I., p. 578.

120   THE SOUTHAMPTON INSURRECTION.

Southern legislation and was the cause of the comparatively slow increase of slaves, especially in the older slave States. Mr. Brackett[1] says: "In the summer of 1793 there arrived in Baltimore, Maryland, some twelve hundred refugees from San Domingo, flying from the horrors of servile insurrection. They brought half as many slaves with them. They were, reported a committee in the Assembly, in a state of distress which exceeded description. The Assembly appropriated five hundred dollars weekly for two months, and thousands of dollars were raised for them throughout the State. The horrors of this insurrection had not been forgotten, when, in the autumn of 1831, there came the report of the revolt of the slaves in Southampton county, Virginia." Similar reports of distress were made to several of the Legislatures of the Southern States, and in response to petitions from these distressed people liberal appropriations were made by the Legislatures, as well as by private persons. The result was soon seen in Virginia. In 1793 the slaves of Northampton and other sections of Eastern Virginia showed signs of discontent. The Gabriel Prosser insurrection, which occurred in Richmond in 1800, was due to French statements that the scenes of St. Domingo might be even more successfully executed in Virginia. Gabriel Prosser's example did much to keep alive the recollections of St. Domingo, and in 1801 and succeeding years rebellious slaves in various sections of Virginia confessed that they had been inspired by hopes that Gabriel's plans and those of the negroes of Hayti might be successfully repeated. This was especially the case immediately preceding and during the war of 1812, when the possibility of English assistance rendered a servile insurrection more certain of success.

[1] The Negro in Maryland, p. 96.

Through these recorded facts, the other attempts at servile insurrection, and the traditions of the refugees, the recollections of St. Domingo were still vivid in 1831.[1] It is probable that the negroes who murdered their masters in Southampton in 1799 circulated reports of this catastrophe. From the investigation of the Governor of Virginia it was found that they had traveled to and from many of the seaports and had ample means of communication with the cooks and other servants of the vessels plying between the United States and the West Indies, and of conversing with the slaves forced aboard vessels by the French refugees. The shrewdness, device, and wickedness of these negroes also seem to indicate the truth of this statement. The abolition papers, too, kept these scenes before the public, and pictured the leaders as heroes.[2] The "Genius of Universal Emancipation," edited by Benjamin Lundy, of Baltimore, gave a detailed history of such affairs in successive numbers in 1828. There was, however, a more direct source. Some of these refugees from St. Domingo settled in Southampton, having brought their negroes with them. Nat being a preacher, freely passing from one section of the country to another, very probably had his dreams fired by the recitals of

[1] In the legislatures, as well as in the foreign correspondence of the United States and petitions to Congress, references were continually made to the Republic of Hayti. This was especially the case in the debates in the Cabinet and Congress in regard to Cuba. The Journals of the Virginia House of Delegates and Senate of 1792, 1804, and 1831-32. Callahan, "Cuba and Anglo-American Relations."

[2] A pamphlet which appeared in 1830 urges the negroes to remember Carthage and Hayti and the manner in which they were oppressed by the whites. After declaring American slavery more cruel and vile than that of Greece or Rome, the author says, "But why need I to refer to antiquity, when Hayti, the glory of the blacks and the terror of tyrants, is enough to convince the most avaricious and stupid of wretches."—Walker's Appeal.

122 THE SOUTHAMPTON INSURRECTION.

events occurring in their former homes. A gentleman,[1] who distinctly remembers the execution of seven of the leaders of Nat's band, says: "I have no recollection of Philip, who came from St. Domingo with my father. From tradition I know him well. Whether he saved my father's life or not is not known to me. I think it likely it was so. I do not recollect having heard in the family that it was so. He seems to have had some disagreement with his wife, became discontented, and left the farm. My father supposed he went to Norfolk and thence made his way to St. Domingo. He never heard from him. It is more than likely that Philip may have had communication with some of those who were ringleaders in the drama—and a bloody one it was—that occurred in our county in 1831. * * * Now, what gave rise to this insurrectionary movement, to what extent it may have been influenced by the St. Domingo affairs, whether Philip's recital of events there may have entered as elements in these commotions, I do not know. I think it likely Nat Turner knew all about them, and think it not unlikely he obtained them from Philip." Another citizen writes: "Denegre came to Southampton from the Island of St. Domingo, making his escape in a small boat, with the assistance of a faithful negro servant, who informed him of the attempted uprising of the negroes. Mr. Denegre, as soon as he landed in the United States, gave this man his freedom, who remained with him some twenty years, and then went back to his old home, the island, and wrote back he had

---

[1] W. O. Denegre (born 1825, left Southampton in 1840), St. Paul, Minn., son of John Denegre, who settled in Southampton in 1793. Mr. John Denegre married a Miss Cobb, a near relative of the chief magistrate who presided at the trial of Nat Turner. He was a merchant at Vicksville, and, in the words of a citizen of the county, "represented the county in the Legislature when it was an honor and none but the most prominent men could be elected."

THE SOUTHAMPTON INSURRECTION. 123

returned."[1] These letters also illustrate the ease of communication between slaves of the United States and the people of the West Indies by means of the negroes and corrupt whites of the vessels plying between the two countries. There were at this time, and had been for some years, organizations for revolutions in Cuba and other West Indian Islands for the purpose of freeing the slaves. In 1822 the negroes of Charleston, South Carolina, were detected in active communication with St. Domingo, and in 1829 there was an insurrection in Antigua. Again in 1830 these influences were seen in an armed attempt at insurrection in South Carolina, which, however, was local and soon put down.

The state of affairs in South America and the neighboring islands was not such as to inspire tranquillity and contentment among the slaves of the United States. "By 1829 all the South American provinces," said Metternich, "had gone the way of the flesh."[2] Peru was the last to go, and Spain was driven to the islands. The example of the United States had been a powerful incentive in the assertion of their independence, and she served their cause by her neutrality. The Southern States considered it a means of gradually driving slavery from their borders. But when these provinces established independent governments, "ideas of the equality of man had spread so rapidly, especially through the influence of England, who felt compelled to make retribution to the negro for the sins of slavery which she had inflicted upon all of her colonies, that they each separately declared the slaves free, and by 1830 there was no slavery from Mexico to Cape Horn, except in Brazil." The presence of free

[1] Captain W. H. Hood, Henderson, North Carolina. He married the granddaughter of Mr. John Denegre.

[2] Autobiography of Metternich, vol. IV, p. 165, et seq. I am indebted to Dr. J. M. Callahan for verifying numerous references in this section on the foreign relations of the United States.

negroes so near the borders of the United States and the British possessions was an encouragement to rebellion on the part of the slaves, yet the United States, in 1822,[1] and England, in 1825, were the first to acknowledge the independence of these States, since they found it practicable to emancipate their slaves and at the same time maintain independence without the protection of some other power.

But the question of the independence of Cuba and the other West Indies was different. Their population was such that it was doubtful whether any of them could maintain their independence except under the protection of some other power. Consequently, England and the United States did not desire any extension of the principles of emancipation, which might endanger their slaveholding interests. The United States especially desired that no negro republics should be established near her shores, and on account of its political constitution she had refused to acknowledge the government of Hayti. Cuba's position made it a special object of concern both to the United States and England, neither of which desired to see it in the possession of any power save Spain. But so long as Cuba remained in the hands of Spain it was open to attacks from Mexico and Colombia, and if conquered by them there was danger of its becoming a bone of contention which would lead to war, during which some foreign power might claim the right to conquer it as well as the two contestants. For this reason England and the United States opposed the contemplated expedition of these two States under Santa Anna, which was intended to arouse the slaves of Cuba against Spain, who was zealously striving to subjugate them. Great Britain and the United States admitted that as belligerents Mexico and Colombia had a right to attack their enemies and cap-

[1]Richardson, Messages and Papers of the Presidents, vol. II, p. 331 et seq.

ture their possessions, but added that they ought to remember that this warfare might be very prejudicial to England and the United States by causing an insurrection of the blacks, and by the pretext which it opened to other nations to interfere in the affairs of Cuba, and perhaps to forcibly occupy the island. The extension of such a servile war was especially threatening to the United States. The St. Domingo rebellion had been felt too sensibly to suppose that the blacks of Cuba would be restrained with less difficulty. For the mulattoes of the French and Spanish colonies were far more numerous and intelligent than those of countries settled by Englishmen. Many of the Southern statesmen feared a Mexican invasion of Cuba more than any European possession of it. Mr. Hamilton, of South Carolina, said that a cession of Cuba to England could not be near so dangerous to the United States as the erection of a second Carthage or Hayti "to shadow our shores."[1]

Besides, there was danger of Spain's calling France to her aid in case of a panic as to the intentions of the United States and England in regard to Cuba. Mr. Canning, therefore, proposed an alliance, by which England, France, and the United States should each disclaim any intention of occupying Cuba, and should protest against such occupation by the others. Mr. King, United States Minister at London, however, thought the omission of any mention of Mexico and Colombia might cause an immediate invasion of Cuba and give rise to questions which would throw the whole West Indies into disorder and perhaps excite much anxiety in the Southern part of the United States, instead of leading to a suspension of hostilities on the part of Spain.[2] France, too, refused to sign

[1] Callahan, "Cuba and Anglo-American Relations": J. Q. Adams' Memoirs; Debates in Congress; Government Documents; Collection of Correspondences in British and Foreign State Papers, vol. 26.
[2] Thirty-two Dispatches (Great Britain), August, 1825.

the agreement, and Canning then proposed signing with the United States alone, but Mr. Clay, Secretary of State, considered it no longer necessary and proper to consider the subject, and stated that after the friendly communication between the British and American Governments, "each must now be considered as much bound to a course of forbearance and abstinence in regard to Cuba and Porto Rico as if they had pledged themselves to it by a solemn act." He also informed the French Government that he could not suppose any European power would attempt to occupy Cuba without the concurrence or knowledge of the United States. His policy was in accord with the "Monroe Doctrine," that America, having made herself free and independent, was not hereafter to be governed by any European power, and that any attempt at this would be regarded by the United States as dangerous to their own peace and safety.

This sympathy with the colonies in revolt caused much friction with the Spanish authorities, who, from fear of his influencing revolts, refused to admit a Consul or agent from the United States to Cuba, though they were unable to protect American commerce against the pirates. This was a subject of much controversy in the Cabinet and Congress and with the public in general, and caused great hostility to Spain in America. Many advocated blockading Cuba and Porto Rico, and privateers were fitted out against the pirates, and, in some cases, very likely, became pirates themselves. Finally both England and the United States claimed and executed the right of pursuing the pirates, who had taken refuge on the coast of Cuba. Still, public sentiment was aroused and Cuba continued an uncertain prize. France, England, Colombia, and Mexico were only held off by fear of each other and of the United States. The latter, though appealed to for assistance by the inhabitants, used her influence to prevent a change in the political condition of Cuba, and was determined that no nation should have it except Spain. For, under any other control, there would have been an attempt at independence and a probable slave insurrection. These dangers were the keys to much statecraft and diplomacy on the part of the United States.[1] Spain continued to oppress Mexico and Colombia for the purpose of forcing England and America to guarantee her the possession of Cuba, and even offered to receive a United States Consul at Havana on this condition, but the United States Government, considering this too great a risk in proportion to the benefits derived, urged Russia to prevail upon Spain to make peace at once if she wished to retain Cuba and Porto Rico. The Mexican Minister at London advocated the propriety of making Cuba independent, under the guaranty of all the American States and Great Britain. Mr. Gallatin wrote Mr. Clay that it was the only policy which could give a permanent security to the United States, and told Mr. Canning that complications in Anglo-American relations might result from an Anglo-Spanish war, especially as to Cuba, which, it is understood, should not fall into the hands of either the United States or England. But the suggestion received no further consideration.

The American policy toward the Panama Congress in 1826 was largely connected with Cuba and slavery.[2] An invasion of Cuba and Porto Rico was stated to be an object of the Congress. It was seen that such an invasion might lead to internal convulsions and a servile war which would endanger the institutions of the Southern

[1] J. Q. Adams' Memoirs; Monroe Papers; Jefferson Papers; Congressional Debates; British and Foreign State Papers, vol. 26; Cuba and Anglo-American Relations; Select Documents of United States History, Macdonald; Messages and Papers of the Presidents, vol. II.

[2] Congressional Debates, March and April, 1826.

States. President Adams[1] favored sending delegates to Panama, as such a step might discourage any project to change the existing conditions in Cuba. The debate was warm in regard to sending delegates, but all parties agreed that they should interfere if any foreign power attempted to take territory contiguous to our shores. They thought that self-preservation compelled us to watch anxiously over Cuba.

In 1829 England put on foot schemes to stir up revolution in Cuba.[2] The Spanish Minister at London in June of that year informed his government that the British had sent a frigate to the Canaries with commissioners to investigate what preparations were being made for an expedition against the new Spanish-American States; that they also went to Havana, where they found many ready to revolt, and that they left emissaries in Cuba "to guide public opinion." By this means England hoped to get possession of the island, either on mortgage for money loaned Spain or by an invitation for protection from the inhabitants of the island. This information caused much uneasiness in the United States, as the report was based on the authority of the Duke of Wellington, who advised a British officer to give immediate notice of any signs of disaffection in Cuba. But England was careful to frustrate all attempts at seizure of the island by any other country. During the year Bolivar had gathered ships and forces at Caracas for a contemplated invasion of Porto Rico, but Mr. Cockburn, the British Minister to Colombia, energetically discouraged such an attempt against any of the Spanish islands and frustrated the plans of Bolivar.

The indemnity treaty which Spain made with Great Britain and France lessened the possibility of interference

[1] Messages and Papers of the Presidents, vol. II, pp. 329, 356, 385.

[2] 33 Dispatches (Spain); 28 Dispatches (Spain); Everett to Clay, August 17, 1827.

in Spanish affairs, but the United States Government did not consider that it entirely obviated the danger of an attempted occupation of Cuba. Thus the United States Minister at Madrid was instructed that, while it was not the American policy to give a direct promise to guarantee Cuba to Spain, the United States would be ready to prevent any blow that might threaten Cuba, or any objectionable project which might affect the affairs of nations in American commerce. The unsuccessful expedition which Spain sent from Cuba against Mexico in 1828 was, however, a cause of some solicitude to the American Government, and Secretary Van Buren stated that, although the government had preserved Cuba to Spain when Mexico and Colombia were ready to strike a blow, and although the possession of Cuba by the new States might give England and France a chance to get it, yet the United States could hardly interfere with a defensive attack which Mexico or Colombia might think it to their interest to make, unless such attack should threaten to disturb the internal condition of the island, or result in measures which would tend to incite the island to revolt. By 1830, when a second attack against Mexico was threatened by Spain, the English Government also ceased to offer any objection to a Mexican defensive expedition against Cuba. But by her weakened condition and by popular sentiment at home Spain was forced to discontinue her attempts for the reconquest of her former colonies on the American Continent. Threatened by revolution within, she was unable to form any satisfactory foreign relations, and in 1833, when her King died, the kingdom was in a precarious condition.[1] Thus the international complications which might have arisen if Spain had been able to continue the war were avoided, and all

[1] 14 Special Instructions; 12 United States Ministers' Instructions; Richardson's Messages and Papers of the Presidents, vol. II.

130 THE SOUTHAMPTON INSURRECTION.

the powers "were content to see Cuba remain in the hands of a nation which had depleted its treasury in an unsuccessful attempt to retain half of the American Continent." But the controversy had produced everlasting effects. Questions had been aroused which could not fail to leave their impress upon the country, slave as well as freeman.

All danger of foreign seizure of Cuba had disappeared, but the influence of her slave population was still great. North and South united to resist the establishment of negro republics near our shores; both saw the danger of a servile war extending to the United States from such a source, but both now rushed into heated disputes concerning the extension of slave territory. In 1827 the United States and Mexico were not on good terms.[1] Poinset, the United States Minister to Mexico, was objectionable to her citizens and had to be recalled. The Mexicans claimed that they ought to make better terms with their kinsmen of the South American republics than with the United States. Texas was also a bone of contention. The United States had given up all claim to it in 1819. But slavery and the increasing cotton industry made Texas a desirable acquisition, especially to the slave States, who wished to maintain the balance of power. Negotiations for its purchase were made successively in 1826,[2] 1829, 1830, and 1833. Mexico freed her slaves in 1829, and the cotton crop of Texas made this institution especially desirable to the great numbers of Americans and Englishmen who had settled there. Consequently, they desired union with the United States. The hostility of the Indians to the United States on the Texas borders, as well as in the Northwest, favored this, and the pursuit of some of these by the United States troops into Mexican territory led the Mexican Government to think it a pre-

[1] Richardson's Messages and Papers of the Presidents, vol. II.
[2] Hurd, Law of Freedom and Bondage, p. 195.

THE SOUTHAMPTON INSURRECTION. 131

tense for aiding the Texans in their revolts. The Texans took advantage of this difficulty and declared themselves independent of Mexico in 1833. The strife was severe, but the Texans were so far successful that the United States recognized the Republic of Texas in 1837, and the recognition by England and France followed in 1839. After much continued and heated controversy, this province was annexed to the United States.[1] These difficulties, in which the Northern and Southern sections were so bitterly opposed, could not fail to attract the attention of the negroes of the South and make the Southern people, in whose midst the evil existed, more determined to suppress rebellion, and those more remote to discount its danger.

Nothing better illustrates the insurrectionary influences brought to bear upon the slaves than the difficulties with the Indians of the South and West. On the 30th of March, 1802, in consideration of a cession of a portion of the Georgia territory, now owned by Alabama and Mississippi, the United States agreed to remove the Indians from the limits of Georgia as soon as possible. Many treaties had been made and many millions of square miles of land purchased, but in 1824 the Creeks and Cherokees refused to sell more. In February, 1825, a treaty was signed at Indian Springs by a few Creek chiefs without the authority of the nation, by which they agreed to cede to the United States all the Creek country in Georgia and a large part of that in Alabama. This treaty was supposed to have been the result of fraud on the part of both the chiefs and the two Georgia commissioners. But Monroe, being unable to hold it from the Senate, and no one there exposing its false character, it was ratified. The Indians rebelled, burnt houses, killed the signers of the

[1] Parliamentary Debates, May 20, 1830; J. Q. Adams' Memoirs, vol. II, p. 347; United States Ministers' Instructions (Mexico), vol. 15; Notes from Mexican Ministers, vol. 6.

treaty, and sent representatives to Washington to protest. President Adams had just been inaugurated, and, concluding that the treaty was unfair, suspended all summary proceedings for enforcing it. The State authorities, however, hastened to take possession of the land and to expel the Creeks in accordance with the terms of the treaty. General Gaines and his troops, who had been sent by the President to persuade the Indians to agree to the terms of the treaty, instead of gaining the expected advice and aid of the Governor and militia, fell into a dispute with the executive, who called upon the Legislature to "stand to your arms," and wrote to Mr. Barbour, Secretary of War, that "President Adams makes the Union tremble on a bauble." In a report to the Legislature it was urged that the time was rapidly approaching when the slave States "must confederate." These expressions evince the influence of the Indian controversy upon the institution of slavery. In compliance with the Governor's proclamation, the Legislature passed a law providing for the distribution of the lands, which were treated as subject solely to State jurisdiction. President Adams informed Troup that surveys must stop until Congress settled the matter. The order was obeyed, but the Governor advised the Legislature that "between States equally independent it is not required of the weaker to yield to the stronger. * * * Between sovereignties the weaker is equally qualified to pass upon its rights."

The Creeks refused to ratify the treaty in accordance with General Gaines' proposal, but sent other representatives to Washington, with whom, in January, 1826, Adams concluded a more favorable treaty. The Senate refusing to ratify it, further negotiations resulted in the entire cession and the withdrawal of the Creeks beyond the Mississippi. Again the State authorities began the distribution of land before the treaty was completed, and on February 17, 1827, Governor Troup was forced to call

THE SOUTHAMPTON INSURRECTION. 133

out the State militia to resist the United States troops. This ended the Georgia dispute for a time, as the Executive did not have the support of Congress, which, on the contrary, sustained Troup.[1]

The Cherokees were more civilized and better organized, and they refused to surrender their lands. They were more like the whites, and had acquired considerable slave property. They, like the Creeks, enjoyed by treaty with the United States a tribal government, owing no allegiance to the State of Georgia, but, by continuous cessions, had reduced their settlements to a mountainous district, where they were governed by a few whites of Indian mixture. In 1825, however, they numbered fifteen thousand souls, inclusive of resident whites and slaves, and possessed a fertile district. Everything tended to fix them as a permanent body within the State. "This very success proved an obstacle to their permanent stay in a white community, while preserving a race distinction." Such States as Maine and New York, which had a small tribal remnant to deal with, found it easy to exert white sway. The North had exterminated the Indians in the various French and Indian wars, and by the time of our narrative had entirely recovered from the sufferings thus endured. At this earlier date the whites of the South were allied with the Indians in their neighborhood against the French. Consequently, the Indians, with their separate government, had increased and prospered and had become so numerous as to be a burden to the South, and to enlist in the maintenance of their rights many sentimental philanthropists, especially from those sections too distant to suffer from such disagreeable neighbors. But the whites in their immediate vicinity

[1]Schouler's History of the United States, which gives ample references on the subject; J. Q. Adams' Memoirs, March, 1824; Hart's Formation of the Union, p. 255; Wilson's Division and Reunion, p. 36.

could not endure the equality of a race who were free from all service and allegiance and who were continually inciting the negroes to rebellion.[1]

Each successive Legislature of Georgia from 1826 passed acts limiting the territory of the Cherokees, and that year declared Indian testimony invalid in Georgia courts. The Indians, foreseeing the storm, and warned by the trouble of the Creeks, made all of their land tribal property, thinking thus more readily to secure the protection of the Federal Government. But the Georgia Legislature annexed a portion of it to two of their counties in order to gradually force the Indians to emigrate. In 1828 the State extended her laws over the territory of the Cherokees, and the next year Alabama and Mississippi followed her example.[2] Jackson, in his first message to Congress, says: "I informed the Indians inhabiting parts of Alabama and Georgia that their attempt to establish an independent government would not be countenanced by the Executive of the United States."[3] He also, at the request of the Governor, withdrew the Federal troops sent to Georgia to protect the Indians. Three times between 1830 and the close of 1832 the claims of the Indians were taken from the Georgia courts to the Supreme Court of the United States, and each time the court declared in favor of the Indians as claimants under treaties with the United States. But the Executive refused to enforce the decisions.

The greatest evil came from the Seminoles, of Florida. They formed a branch of the Creek Nation, but refused to fulfill the treaty of August, 1790, between the United States and the Creeks, by which they agreed to surrender

[1]Columbus (Ga.) Compiler of September 8, 1831.
[2]Hart, Formation of the Union.
[3]Messages and Papers of the Presidents, vol. II; Niles Register; Sumner's Jackson.

all slaves who had fled to them. It was for this reason that the treaty of Indian Springs stipulated for the liquidation of the claims of Georgia for damages to property robbed and destroyed previous to 1802, provided the sum did not exceed $250,000. The depredations continued, and, under the French and Spanish sway in Florida, they were especially troublesome, partly on account of the inability of the authorities to overcome them and partly on account of foreigners inciting the Indians against the United States. Jackson marched against them in 1818, and for this reason felt justified in disregarding the neutral rights of Spain on the Florida peninsula, and in hanging two British subjects. At this time more than one thousand slaves had taken refuge among the Indians, with whom they had intermarried and formed a dangerous horde on the outskirts of the slave States, constantly inciting the slaves to rebellion.[1] This continued the case, notwithstanding article vii of the treaty of Camp Moultrie, September 18, 1823, which obligated the Seminoles to "use all necessary exertions to apprehend and deliver the same (absconding slaves or fugitives from justice) to the agent."[2]

On the 9th of May, 1832, another treaty, fraudulent, some say,[3] was signed by some of the Seminole chiefs, agreeing to investigate the lands west of the Mississippi, and if they found them satisfactory and the Creeks willing to reunite with them, to vacate Florida by 1835. The

[1] An address of prominent citizens of Florida to the President reads: "While these indomitable people continue where they now are, the owners of slaves in our territory and even in the States contiguous cannot, for a moment, in anything like security, enjoy this kind of property."—Von Holst, Constitutional History of the United States, vol. II, p. 294; Gidding's Speeches, p. 8; Executive Documents, Twenty-fifth Congress, Third Session, No. 225, p. 56.
[2] Statutes at Large, VII, p. 225.
[3] Niles, LVI, p. 289; Memoirs of J. Q. Adams, IX, p. 518.

commissioners were satisfied with what they found, and the Indians signed a supplementary treaty at Fort Gibson on the 28th of March, 1833, in which they promised to begin to migrate "as soon as the government will make arrangements for them satisfactory to the Seminole Nation."[1] The negroes feared the Creeks, however, who claimed them in compensation for the residue of the $250,000 which had been left after paying the Georgia claims, and which Congress had refused them. Thus the negroes determined to frustrate the execution of the treaty. In 1834 Governor Duval expressed his conviction that the removal of the Indians would be impossible until the negroes were mastered. These Indians and negroes were especially dangerous, as they could fall back into the malarial swamps, which furnished the products needed by them, but whose climate was deadly to the white man.[2] Eager to recapture their slaves and force a fulfillment of the treaty, the citizens, aided by the government officials, advanced into this country and recklessly seized the negroes, among whom was the wife of a chief, Osceola, a half-breed. The latter raged and was only calmed by his desire to escape prison and later wreak vengeance on his captors. He proceeded to the swamps and formed one of the most bloody plots. The United States agent in Florida was massacred, with several of his friends, and Major Dade, with one hundred troops, was attacked and only one man escaped to tell the story.[3] Indians and negroes assembled on all sides, murdered citizens, and burned plantations promiscuously. It was impossible to subdue them, having been made desperate by their inability, as on former occasions, to retire before the encroachments of the whites.

[1] Statutes at Large, VII, pp. 423, 424.
[2] Niles Register, LVII, p. 314.
[3] Ibid, XLIX, p. 367.

In March, 1837, General Jesup concluded a treaty with the Indians at Camp Dade,[1] from which he expected an end of the war.[2] In order to prevent interference by the whites with the negro property of the Indians, and to assist their emigration, he issued, on April 5th, an army order prohibiting all whites not engaged in the service of the United States from entering the territory between the St. John river and the Gulf of Mexico south of Fort Dane. The citizens of East Florida protested that this was protecting the Indians in their depredations upon the white inhabitants, and that no pacification could result from the order. On April 8th General Jesup persuaded the chiefs to surrender all the negroes of the whites that had fled to them before the beginning of the war,[3] and on the 27th promised not to let those that had absconded before it leave the country.[4] The negroes took alarm and fled to the swamps. Jesup confessed, "All is lost, and, principally, I fear, by the influence of the negroes and of the people who were the subject of our correspondence."[5] The contest was renewed with vigor. The soldiers were to have the property of the Seminoles that fell into their hands. The Creeks were offered inducements to join the forces of the United States, besides the property that fell into their possession and a reward of twenty dollars per

[1] Executive Documents, Twenty-fifth Congress, Third Session, vol. V, No. 225, pp. 52, 53.

[2] He writes at this time: "There is no disposition on the part of the greater body of the Indians to renew hostilities, and they will, I am sure, faithfully fulfill their engagements if the inhabitants of the territory be prudent, but any attempt to seize their negroes or other property would be followed by an instant resort to arms. I have some hopes of inducing both the Indians and the Indian negroes to unite in bringing in the negroes taken from the citizens during the war." Executive Documents, Twenty-fifth Congress, Third Session, vol. V, No. 225, p. 9.

[3] Executive Documents, Twenty-fifth Congress, Third Session, vol. V, No. 225, pp. 10, 108, 109.

[4] Ibid, p. 13.

[5] Jesup to Colonel Gadesden, June 14, 1837.

138 THE SOUTHAMPTON INSURRECTION.

head for each negro captured. This last was to induce the Indians to take alive and not destroy the negroes of the citizens who had been captured by the Seminoles. The consequence of this policy was that within a short time most of the negroes had been captured. The Indians, however, continued so strong that Jesup recommended that they should be left in Florida for a time and confined to a definite district.[1] But this proposition was rejected,[2] and the war continued.

In March, 1839, Congress appropriated $5,000 to conclude a treaty with the Seminoles,[3] and the President sent General Macomb to Florida to endeavor to bring about peace. The reconciliation which he accomplished, however, was indefinite and ambiguous on the decisive subject.[4] Not only the Seminoles, but the whites understood the agreement to mean that the Indians were promised to be allowed to remain for an indefinite time. Treachery on both sides was the signal for the renewal of the war after a few weeks, which continued until armed occupation by white settlers brought to a close the last serious obstacle to the national policy of transferring the Indians beyond the Mississippi. In pursuance of this policy land was offered free to those settlers who would reside five years in Florida. In great numbers people flocked hither, bringing their plows and other implements for clearing the forests. They established lines of defense, and soon the Seminoles were reduced to about three hundred, who were allowed to reside within the limits in the lower marshes of the peninsula.

It would appear at first thought that these Indian wars exerted a more injurious effect upon the slaves after 1831 than before. But the reverse was the case. Previous to

[1] Jesup to Poinset, February 11, 1838, Niles, LIV.
[2] Poinset to Jesup, March 1, 1838, Niles, p. 52.
[3] Statutes at Large, vol. V, p. 358; Niles, vol. LVII, p. 313.
[4] Niles, vol. LVI, p. 249.

this date the issues were only partisan, and the most stringent measures to prevent insurrection had not been deemed necessary. The principles which dominated the policy of the United States as to Cuba and the West Indies now controlled the slave section in regard to the Indians, the Administration of Jackson concurring so far as to foresee more danger from this source than from the doctrine of nullification which he later bitterly opposed in the case of South Carolina and the tariff.[1] But in those parts of the country remote from the slave and Indian population there arose a sympathy for the Indian race, like that for the negro, strongest in those States which were unembarrassed by its neighborhood. Black Hawk, the bold, crafty leader of the Winnebagoes, Sacs and Foxes, was extolled as a hero and general. Osceola, bloodthirsty and perfidious, was exalted into a patriot. The expression of these sympathies was only one step in advance of the hostilities first begun in the Missouri Compromise. Thus these Indian wars had a two-fold effect, both in encouraging the slaves to rebellion and in arousing sympathy for the negro in the sentimental abolitionist, who worked for the same end.

The abolition societies and Quakers, as early as 1789, petitioned Congress to abolish slavery. But all minds were put at ease for many years by the declaration that slavery was a question to be regulated by the individual States. During this era of peace, domestic and foreign, Virginia exerted every effort to free her slaves, but was

[1] The people of Florida saw the evil and said: "The contiguity of the emancipated colored population of the West Indies would, in a war with some foreign power, place Florida and, in fact, the whole of our Southern States, in jeopardy. There is no position in which those Indians could be located so dangerous to the peace and happiness of the Southern people and interests of the United States as the peninsula of Florida."—Niles, vol. LVI, pp. 265, 266.

140   THE SOUTHAMPTON INSURRECTION.

confronted with the problem of what to do with them when free. The North had gradually freed hers, compensating the owners therefor, and all economic interest in the institution having been lost, a strong abolition sentiment sprang up which was destined to prevent Virginia's accomplishing the same end in the same manner.[1] The movement took a new turn in the form of forged petitions, signed by fictitious names of negroes, and did not, as the old Quaker one of earlier date, "respect constitutional bounds and seek mild persuasion of the white master who held the local law in his hands. It boldly proclaimed that the laws of nature were paramount to a human institution; it preached freedom as of divine right, and in defiance, if need be, of the enslavers. * * * Abolitionism slid into an angry tirade against the Constitution as a covenant with death and agreement with hell, and their creed became 'no union with slaveholders.' * * * We shall see in the angry years that follow the Southern secessionists and Northern abolitionists standing upon essentially the same platform, though at opposite ends, both demanding that the American Union be broken up."[2]

So great had the sentiment grown by 1826 that, in

[1]Mr. Benton said in the United States Senate in 1835 that the abolition societies had thrown the state of the emancipation question fifty years back and subjected every traveler and every immigrant from non-slave-holding States to be received with coldness and viewed with suspicion and jealousy in the slaveholding States; further, that they had occasioned many slaves to lose their lives, caused the privileges of slaves to be curtailed and their bonds to be more tightly drawn, besides opening a gulf of misery to the free people of color.

It is well to note here that by abolitionists is meant not those who favored emancipation provided the negroes were sent beyond the limits of the United States, but those who demanded the unconditional abolition of slavery. The latter by no means comprised the majority of Northern people, while the former class embraced many influential slave-holders of the South.

[2]Schouler's History of the United States, vol. IV, pp. 210, 211.

response to a petition from Francis Larche, Mr. Martindale, from the Committee on Claims of the House, made the following report: "That this is a claim for the value of a slave belonging to the petitioner, impressed into the service of the United States by General Jackson in the defense of New Orleans, and alleged to have been killed by a cannon shot while in service. Without stopping to deny or admit any of the facts by which the petitioner supports any of his claims, the committee recommends its rejection upon principle. The emergency justifies the impressing of every moral agent capable of contributing to the defense of the place; to call upon the master to defend himself and slave, as well as the slave to defend his master. It would be the height of injustice to call upon the free citizens of States many miles distant from the place assaulted to pour out their blood and sacrifice their lives for its defense and at the same time to exonerate from that service its own physical and moral force. Men are wanted, and in that capacity the slave was put in requisition. The master, too, might have been called upon, and his son, and his hired servants, as they were in other parts of the country, and where sons and fathers and husbands died without their lives being valued or compensated in money." The Southern citizens were accused of desiring pay for slaves lost in the defense of their country, which they refused to defend. But more, the report acknowledged the right of the United States to draft the slaves into service. France had required each province in Hayti to furnish so many negro and mulatto soldiers. The result was well known. Coming just after the Missouri Compromise, the first step which had opened the eyes of the South as to the position of the North, this report thoroughly alarmed Virginia as to the dangers of negro rebellion. The French negroes had been aroused to insurrection by white citizens, and the same danger confronted the South if the doctrine here set forth was once put into operation.[1]

By 1829 not even the broad-minded Webster, who acknowledged that the slave owners were as upright and honest Christians as any in the world, was able to avert the sectional drift of the Public Land question without exhibiting his opposition to slavery and introducing topics which gave a more sectional phase to the debate. He claimed for the "North and the North alone" the credit of the first law passed against slavery, the anti-slavery clause of the Ordinance of 1787, notwithstanding the fact that the honor belonged as much to Virginia, and took Ohio and Kentucky for examples, the superior improvement and population of the former being attributed to the exemption from the evils of slavery. The words of Ben-

---

[1] L. W. Tazewell, one of the Virginia representatives, sent this report to Governor John Tyler, who replied as follows: "Your favor of the 24th of April, covering the report of a committee of the House of Representatives on the subject of Larche's claims, etc., came duly to hand, and but for the correction, which, I trust, may be found in the good sense in the House of Representatives, would be well calculated to excite the most gloomy forebodings.

"We should, indeed, have reached a point of the most frightful apprehensions when the Congress be found mad enough to sanction the principles, or, more properly, the *non-principles*, contained in the report. It will be a point from which there will be receding and no advancing. But the precedents, fortunately, are all the other way. The late treaty with England, if anything more than the common sense of mankind was wanting to settle this question, does settle it. Slaves are there placed on the footing of *property*, and he must be a wretched and unreliable enthusiast who would question the correctness of that decision. I always thought that certain politicians had gone a bow-shot too far when they attempted, as in this question, to elevate to the condition of *citizens* the free blacks, but Mr. Martindale and his committee, in their notion of *men* and moral *agents*, have made a new and unforeseen discovery. This is what you properly call it, a great question—a question big with the fate of the Union, a principle which startles, and is well calculated to alarm all the sensibilities of the patriot, and one in the settlement of which I shall, along with yourself and our common constituents, watch with the deepest interest."

THE SOUTHAMPTON INSURRECTION. 143

ton in the famous debate will illustrate the hostile and inflammatory language and efforts employed during this period, both in and out of Congress. He says: "Christ saw all of this (the slavery of the ancients) and their white color, which was the same with His own, yet He said nothing against slavery, He preached no doctrines which led to insurrection and massacre, none which, in their application to the state of things in our country, would authorize an inferior race to exterminate that superior race of whites, in whose ranks He Himself appeared upon earth."[1]

Virginia never universally favored slavery, and never lost the hope of some day ridding herself of it. But this hostile sentiment forced her, with the rest of the South, to place herself in a position to be wrongly judged.[2] She saw the result of the discussion of slavery by the French Legislature, and felt that on this question the North bore the same relation to the South as France to St. Domingo. Consequently, her Representatives opposed the right of petitioning Congress on the subject of slavery. This position taken by the South against the right of petition was so favorable to the anti-slavery party that by 1831 the abolitionists had become very powerful in the United States. Alexander's History of African Colonization says:[3] "About this time the zeal of the abolitionists had become exceedingly warm, and great excitement was produced both at the North and the South by the publication of inflammatory pamphlets containing highly colored

[1] Benton, vol. 1, chapter XLIV, pp. 130-137.
[2] Mr. Benton said in 1829 in the United States Senate: "I can truly say that slavery, in the abstract, has but few advocates or defenders in the slave-holding States, and that slavery, as it is, an hereditary institution, descended upon us from our ancestors, would have fewer advocates among us than it has if those who have nothing to do with the subject would only let us alone."
[3] The Virginia History of African Colonization, p. 27.

descriptions of the cruelties exercised toward the slaves in the Southern States, and caricatures were prepared calculated to make a strong impression on the imagination of the people. A pamphlet was printed in Boston, written by one Mr. Walker,[1] which actually aimed to excite the slaves to insurrection, and did not hesitate to exhort them to take vengeance on their owners by imbuing their hands in their blood. Copies of these pamphlets were sent by mail into the Southern country."

Walker says in the preface to this pamphlet: "All I ask is a candid and careful perusal of this the third and last edition of my appeal, where the world may see that we, the blacks or colored people, are treated more cruelly by the white Christians of America than devils themselves ever treated a set of men, women and children on this earth. It is expected that all colored men, women and children of every nation, language and tongue under heaven, will try to procure a copy of the appeal and read it, or get someone to read it to them." He counsels care and courage in attempts at freedom. "Never make an attempt to gain our freedom or national right, from under cruel oppressors and murderers, until you see your way clear. * * * Fear not the number and education of our *enemies*, against whom we shall have to contend for our lawful rights. * * * One good black man can put to death six white men. * * * the whites have always been an unjust, jealous, unmerciful, avaricious and bloodthirsty set of beings always seeking after power and authority." He traces the history of the white race, and declares that they have always acted more like devils

---

[1]This David Walker was a free negro of Boston, and his pamphlet is entitled "Walker's Appeal, in Four Articles, together with a Preamble to the Colored Citizens of the World, but in particular and very expressly to those of the United States of America." It was written September, 1829, and revised and published in 1830. He was a publisher and seems to have devoted his life to arousing the negroes of America.

than accountable men. "If you commence," he continues, "make sure work—do not trifle for they will not trifle with you—they want us for their slaves and think nothing of murdering us in order to subject us to that wretched condition—therefore, if there was an *attempt* made by us, kill or be killed." In August, 1829, a gang of slaves who were being driven through Kentucky rebelled and killed two of the negroes who had charge of them and fled. The third driver was assisted by one of the women to escape. Walker accuses this woman of being ignorant and a server of the devil, and says: "Any person who will save such wretches from destruction is fighting against the Lord, and will receive his just recompense." The negroes are advised to study and surpass the ignorant whites of the South, of whom he declared: "It is a fact that in all our slave-holding States there are thousands of the whites who are almost as ignorant in comparison as horses, the most they know is to beat the colored people, which some of them shall have their heart full of yet. * * * This country is as much ours as it is the whites', whether they will admit it now or not, they will see and believe it by and by." The negroes are warned against the efforts of the Colonization Society as schemes of the slave-holders to get rid of the influences of the free blacks upon the slaves. He pleads for unity, secrecy, and courage, as God would raise up a Hannibal for them if they would only help themselves. This, he feels confident, will be the case some day, as in most of the slave countries the negroes were in the majority and more worthy than the whites. Four hundred and fifty thousand of the five or six hundred thousand negroes in Virginia, well armed, he would put against every white man on the continent of America. His warning to the whites is: "Remember, Americans, that we must and shall be free and enlightened as you are. Will you wait until we shall, under God, obtain our liberty by the crushing arm of force? Will it not be dreadful for you? I speak, Americans, for your good. We must and shall be free, I say, in spite of you. You may do your best to keep us in wretchedness and misery, to enrich you and your children, but God will deliver us from under you. And woe, woe will be unto you if we have to obtain our freedom by fighting. Throw away your fears and prejudices, then, and enlighten us and treat us like men, and we will like you more than we do now hate you."

The General Colored Association of Massachusetts exerted every effort to incite rebellion.[1] It urged negroes to remain in America and work for the cause of emancipation. Richard Allen, a Bishop of the African Methodist Episcopal Church, wrote to the editor of the Freedom's Journal: "I have been for several years trying to reconcile my mind to the colonization of Africa in Liberia, but there have always been and there still remain great and insurmountable objections against the scheme. * * * This land which we have watered with our tears and our *blood* is now our *mother country*, and we are well satisfied to stay where wisdom abounds and the Gospel is free."[2] These negroes were valuable agents for the abolitionists, the principal of whom was William L. Garrison, the editor of the Liberator. Even the poet Whittier wrote a poem entitled "The Branded Hand," of which the following is a stanza:

"And the tyrants of the slaveland shall tremble at that sign,
When it points its finger southward along the Puritan line;

[1] The Freedom's Journal, of December 20, 1828, has an address before the Society by David Walker.
[2] Freedom's Journal, for November 2, 1827, vol. 1, No. 34. They seem to have been very successful.

Woe to the State-gorged leeches and the church's locust band,
When they look from slavery's ramparts on the coming of that hand."[1]

In Baltimore was published the weekly Genius of Universal Emancipation, edited by Benjamin Lundy, which took as its motto, "We hold these truths to be self-evident: that all men are created equal and endowed by their Creator with certain inalienable rights; that among these are life, liberty, and the pursuit of happiness." These organs kept in touch with European affairs and published weekly accounts of them, especially of the abolition movement in England, as given by the (London) Anti-Slavery Monthly Register.

By degrees serfdom disappeared from the social order of Western Europe, leaving the germ of hostility to every form of servitude. England, at an early date, joined with the United States and France in suppressing the slave trade. Spain and Portugal were the last to yield, the former in 1830 and the latter in 1820. In 1823 the English Anti-Slavery party was formed by men like Wilberforce, Buxton, and Macaulay, who secured the passage of a resolution on the 5th of May that the home government recommend to the Colonial Legislatures certain measures of amelioration in the treatment of the slaves, and that, if they refused, these measures be forced upon them. This acquiescence of the home government in the principles of the Anti-Slavery party very much incensed the planters, who took active steps to conceal from the slaves the arrival of the order in council. A vain attempt in Demerara[2] led the slaves to believe they had been set free.

[1]The trial and imprisonment of Jonathan Walker at Pensacola, Florida.
[2]One of the most populous and wealthy provinces of British Guiana. It takes its name from a river running through it.

They refused to work and resisted when force was used. Martial law, however, was proclaimed and the uprising suppressed with great severity. This act excited much indignation in England against the planters, and Wilberforce, Stephen, Brougham, and others abated their efforts only during a period allowed the local Legislatures for carrying into effect the measures expected of them. In 1828 the free people of color were put on a footing of legal equality with the whites. In 1830, since it was evident that the planters did not intend to take further steps for the liberation of the slaves, the leaders in Parliament determined to urge the entire abolition of slavery at the earliest practicable period. This opportunity arrived in 1833, under the Ministry of Lord Grey, and slavery was abolished throughout the British Empire, all slave-holders being paid for the slaves save the Boers of South Africa, who, in consequence, emigrated from Cape Colony and founded the Transvaal, England's eternal enemy. This English anti-slavery zeal was infused into the movement in America by the abolitionists, who dared to import anti-slavery orators from the nation that, above all others, had, from the Revolutionary War on, disturbed the institution of American slavery. This influence was felt to such an extent by 1830 that it could be said: "The English are the best friends the colored people have upon earth. Though they have oppressed us a little and have colonies now in the West Indies which oppress us sorely, yet, notwithstanding, they (the English) have done one hundred times more for the melioration of our condition than all the other nations of the earth put together. The blacks cannot but respect the English as a nation, notwithstanding they have treated us a little cruel."[1] Every-

[1] Walker's Appeal, p. 47.

THE SOUTHAMPTON INSURRECTION. 149

thing was done by the British officials to offend the slaveholders of the United States.¹

These inflammatory papers and pamphlets and reports of affairs abroad were circulated through the mails to such an extent and had such an effect upon the negroes that the State authorities had to take active measures to prevent it.² Nor was this all. Ministers visited Virginia, and instead of preaching the gospel, secretly communi-

¹The Jamaica Courent, of August 26, 1831, says: "We transcribe from the opposition journal recently established at Nassau an article relating to the manner in which the British Government has disposed of certain slaves of the United States, who had been wrecked on their passage from one part of the republic to another and had been brought before the admiralty jurisdiction of the Bahama Islands. According to international law one nation has no right to legislate over a people of another depressed by accident of nature. Such an act comes with very ill-grace from Great Britain, which from the first of William III. to the middle of George III. declared the slave trade to be most beneficial and not to be restrained—nay, forbid her then colonies New Hampshire and Virginia in any way to restrict the trade." After further portraying the manner in which British despotism forced slavery on America when too weak to resist her, and how Jefferson, as acknowledged by Lord Brougham, first effectually raised his voice in inducing Virginia to abolish the slave trade, this paper adds: "Since the United States has been gradually freeing themselves from the internal slave trade and slavery which is acknowledged to be inferior to all classes. She has abolished it in all States north of the Potomac and without violating the rights of her citizens, but with the most equitable consideration of the claims of private property. She proceeded in the natural order, freed from war duties in the time of peace and (with) the certainty of enjoying one's profits of labor, (she) encouraged free labor, which (was) found so much more beneficial than slavery, which never was advantageous except to white Europeans who stole the slaves to sell to the New World. Thus Great Britain forced slavery on her weak colonies, and when they ceased to be hers she finds out the property she sold and created is so base that it justifies a violation of international law."

²A letter from Raleigh to the National Gazette of October 13, 1831, says that a number of the "Liberators," printed in Boston by the editor, William Lloyd Garrison and published by Isaac Knapp, came to Raleigh, and the attorney general submitted an indictment to the grand jury, who found it a "true bill."

cated with the slaves and sent back to the North most horrible accounts of heathenism and cruelties. These men usually were of an inferior type and were aided by other secret agents as peddlers, etc., even women condescending to become abolition missionaries.[1]

A white man, Bradley, was known to have been very intimate with Nat Turner. This fact, together with contemporaneous circumstances, leaves no doubt but that abolition documents and agents had great influence upon the insurrection.[2] In his message to the Legislature in relation to the massacre, Governor Floyd said: "From the documents which I lay before you, there is too much reason to believe those plans of treason, insurrection, and murder have been designed, planned, and matured by unrestrained fanatics in some of the neighboring States, who find facilities in distributing their views and plans

---

[1] The following is an extract from a letter to a gentleman in Norfolk, dated Cambridge, Maryland, October 4, 1831: "A white woman was arrested at Northwest Fork Bridge (22 miles from here). A black man communicated to Representatives Dr. Nicholas and Mr. Kenon that a woman from Philadelphia was sent to instruct the negroes how they might succeed in their conspiracy. He told them he knew he was not a witness against a white person, but that, if they would come to his house that evening, they could hear for themselves. They did so and heard what she had to say; she told the black men if they wanted arms to write on to the Bishop of Bethlemite Church in Philadelphia and he would furnish them with such advice as they should want in their undertaking. She was lodged in jail for trial." This occurred a few months after the Southampton massacre, but it sufficiently illustrates what was going on before this incident.

[2] A letter from Winton, North Carolina, to the Norfolk Herald, dated August 24, 1831, reads: "We are all in a state of confusion here. There has been an insurrection of the negroes of Southampton in the neighborhood of Cross Keys, about thirty miles from here. From the best information we have had, three white men and four slaves of a gentleman near Cross Keys rose upon him before day on Monday and killed him and all his white family," etc. "He (Nat) had been influenced by religious fanaticism and by white preachers of black equality."—Stephen B. Weeks in Magazine of American History for 1897.

THE SOUTHAMPTON INSURRECTION. 151

among our population either through the postoffice or by agents sent for that purpose throughout our territory." These agents were especially accessible to the free negroes and through them to the slaves. After portraying further influence of these agents, the Governor continues: "Some proof is also furnished that for the class of free people of color they have offered more enlarged views and urge the achievement of a higher destiny by means, for the present, less violent, but not differing in the end from those presented to the slaves."[1] Mr. R. A. Brock writes: "The fruits of these incendiary machinations soon began to appear. On the 21st and 22d of August, 1831, a body of sixty or seventy slaves, under the leadership of Nat Turner, the slave of Mr. Benjamin Turner, of Southampton, arose on the white inhabitants of the county and butchered by night fifty-five persons, chiefly helpless women and children."[2]

GENERAL CHARACTER OF THE INSURRECTION.—The Southampton insurrection was barbarous beyond degree. Depredations, murder, and the most revolting crimes were committed in cold blood, but its true nature and extent have never been thoroughly grasped. Either it is represented as having been confined to a portion of a magisterial district, or its leader is said to have recruited his forces through all Eastern Virginia and Carolina south of James river. The former view is of later origin and due to the words of Nat Turner and to a desire to believe the disaffection of limited extent and uninfluenced by external events. Having assured Nat of

[1] Mr. Collin Kitchen was in Smithfield when he heard the news of the insurrection. He at once started for home. But at the Blackwater the Isle of Wight troops refused his passage for some time, as they feared he was a pretended trader lending aid to the insurgents. They had moved the planks of the bridge in order to more readily resist the passage of white spies.

[2] Collections of the Virginia Historical Society, New Series, vol. VI.

the certain death that awaited him, and convinced him that concealment would only bring destruction on the innocent as well as the guilty of his own color, Mr. Gray asked him if he knew any extensive or concerted plan. His answer was, "I do not." He denied all knowledge of a similar rebellion in North Carolina, and added: "I see, sir, you doubt my word: but can you not think the same ideas and strange appearances about this time in the heavens might prompt others, as well as myself, to this undertaking?" It was but natural, on the other hand, that the extent of the plot should be exaggerated. In the summer of 1831 there were slave revolts in Martinique, Antigua, St. Jago (Santiago), Caracas, and Tortugas. Their influence seems to have spread to the United States. In Delaware and Maryland there were signs of discontent among the slaves, mostly caused by slave dealers, who stirred up discontent among the slaves in order to induce the masters to sell them at low rates, and in many cases induced the slaves to flee in the hope of promised freedom and a life of ease and comfort, free from work.[1] A letter[2] from Princess Anne, Somerset county, Maryland, says: "Much excitement prevails from an apprehended insurrection of the negroes; patrols have been out for several nights in all parts of the county, and several high characters have been brought in and committed to prison." The slaves working the gold mines of Burke and Rutherford counties, North Carolina, were discovered in a deep-laid plot. A letter[3] from Rutherfordton says: "The negroes working the mines of the neighborhood have been detected in insurrectionary attempts and several brought before the Supreme Court, one general, a major, two captains, and others of inferior grade. The best white people

[1] These men sold the same negroes in the extreme Southern States for large sums.
[2] Baltimore Patriot.
[3] National Gazette, October 13, 1831.

THE SOUTHAMPTON INSURRECTION. 153

have been called together to take measures to suppress the insurrectionary spirit and prevent the introduction of mean negroes." In Richmond county several arrests were made and iron spikes for carrying into execution the scheme of the slaves were discovered.

The entire Black Belt seems to have been aroused. The first information of this was reported to Mr. Usher, of South Washington, by a free negro, who said that Dave, a slave of Mr. Morisey, of Sampson, solicited his co-operation and that of several others in an insurrection. Mr. Usher communicated this information to Mr. Kelly, of Duplin, who immediately caused the arrest of Dave. He confessed to his master that the negroes of Sampson, Duplin, Lenoir, and New Hanover were regularly organized and prepared to rise on the 4th of October, and he gave the names of the four leaders in Sampson and Duplin and of several in Wilmington. Having murdered the principal families, the insurgents intended marching upon Wilmington by two routes. Here they expected a reinforcement of two thousand, after which, well armed, they were to return and take possession of the country. Troops were called out in every county in the State and the greatest excitement prevailed. On September 13th the citizens of Sampson county wrote the Governor: "Sir: The inhabitants of Sampson have been alarmed with an insurrection of the negroes. We have ten or fifteen negroes in jail and have such proof that most of them will be bound over to our Superior Court. We have testimony that will implicate most of the negroes in the county. We wish you to issue an order to the colonel of the county to appoint a guard to guard the jail until the negroes shall have their trial. The people of Duplin county have examined ten or fifteen negroes and found two guilty and have put them to death. There never was such excitement in Sampson and Duplin before." A dispatch from Washington to Wilmington represented the negroes two hundred strong as marching from the former to the latter place. A second dispatch confirmed this report, and the citizens flew to arms. The females collected in houses near the courthouse and remained in anxious sleeplessness until daylight brought the tidings that the report was false and that the firing heard and supposed to be an encounter between the whites and blacks was nothing more than a discharge from a swivel by some young men at Lisburn (Black River), with the intention of clearing it out. The blacks had never assembled with any treasonable intent, and the companies that turned out in the neighboring counties merely pursued thirty or forty negroes, who had fled from fright. In Raleigh a report was circulated that the negroes, having burned Wilmington, were marching upon the capital. The entire night of September 12th was spent under arms, and the morning of the 13th presented a dreary aspect. The leading men assembled in the courthouse to examine suspected negroes, while women ran, distracted, in every direction. All business was suspended, and the arms and ammunition of the stores were confiscated. All the males enlisted in companies, even the old men forming the "Silver Greys," and fortified the churches and other public buildings, to which the women and children were to flee at the first sound of the capitol bell. Such was the state of affairs, when a gentleman from Johnson county rushed into the town appealing for arms and ammunition.[1] It was reported that twenty-one negroes had been arrested in Edenton on a charge of inciting rebellion, that Clinton had been burned, and the bridge over the Cape Fear river at Fayetteville blown up. The tension of the citizens was at such a pitch that when O'Rouke's blacksmith shop took fire the capitol bell tolled and the alarm spread. "Nat Turner and his followers are upon us!" The negroes

[1] His horse fell dead as he dismounted.

THE SOUTHAMPTON INSURRECTION. 155

were even more alarmed than the whites. On the 14th every free negro was examined before the committees of vigilance, and those that could not give a satisfactory account of their means of subsistence were either imprisoned or ordered to leave the place forthwith. The slaves were also carefully examined and every kitchen searched. The alarm soon subsided, however, and the negroes in general "behaved manfully, and caused a high reputation for disinterested intrepidity and strict honesty."[1] To avoid suspicion, those negroes who were on their way to market, as soon as they heard of the insurrection, left their goods at the nearest farmhouses and returned home to report to their masters. These facts, together with the report that the negroes of the counties of North Carolina contiguous to Southampton contemplated rebelling on the same day with those of that county, and had failed in this resolve merely from a misunderstanding, there being five Sundays in August instead of four, naturally led to the belief that the Southampton insurrection was general and extended over all Carolina and Virginia.

Both of the views given are in a measure tiue. The influence of the insurrection was widespread, extending to the North as well as to the South.[2] The negroes of North Carolina were encouraged by the partial success of Nat Turner, but the disturbed spirit of the slaves was a natural consequence of the times, and seems to have been

[1]The American Annual Register said this in commendation of the negroes of Fayetteville at the $1,500,000 fire in May, 1831.

[2]Rev. Lorenzo Dow, in his "Life and Works," p. 159, says: "The negro plot of General Nat in Virginia, extended from the State of Delaware to the Gulf of Mexico, systematically arranged, as is evident from the various executions in a string, about that time, exemplified in various places! Also the foreigners, systematically itinerating for what purpose, antecedent and subsequent to that time. Moreover, it is evident the slaves could not have had the opportunity of such systematical arrangement, so extensive; hence it is evident that it must be traced to another source—white men behind the scene.

156 THE SOUTHAMPTON INSURRECTION.

greatest in that portion of Carolina most accessible to external influences, and which it was impossible for the direct exertion of the Southampton negroes to reach. On the other hand, though the execution of the plot was confined to a magisterial district of three thousand inhabitants, every effort was exerted to arouse the negroes of the neighboring counties of Virginia and Carolina. General Eppes, in a general order, and again in an official letter, to the Governor, reported that he was convinced from various sources that there existed no general concert among the slaves, and that circumstances, impossible to have been feigned, demonstrated the entire ignorance on the subject of all the slaves of the counties around Southampton. The editor of the Norfolk Herald, however, in the number which contained this expression of General Eppes' opinion, says that there were divers reports that favored the idea of a preconcerted plan of operation extending to other counties, in which a number of implicated negroes were on trial. In September a negro preacher was arrested in Prince William, and the Petersburg Intelligencer of the second Friday in September says: "In Prince George, on Thursday last, a slave of the name of Christopher, belonging to Mr. Henry C. Heath, a blacksmith by trade and a preacher by profession, was tried by the county court on a charge of being connected with the Southampton conspirators, and condemned to death. He is to be hung the first Friday in October." In October several negroes confined in Sussex jail knocked the jailer down and attempted to escape. Only one succeeded. One was killed, one wounded, and four, captured by the guard, were tried and executed.[1] Thus four negroes were condemned and two transported by Sussex for connection with the Southampton insurrection, while Nansemond transported one and Surry one.

[1] National Gazette, November 1, 1831.

THE SOUTHAMPTON INSURRECTION. 157

Similar results seem to have been the consequence in other counties. A gentleman of Nansemond says: "I have often been told that the plans for the insurrection were laid at Barnes' Church, at a protracted meeting, the Sunday preceding the night the conspirators commenced their cruel work. I have also often heard that there were a great many negroes from around Winton, North Carolina, and other places quite a distance from the church. I have often been told by my mother, who lived in Nansemond county, about four miles from the Southampton county line, and more than twenty miles from this (Barnes') church, that an old negro (Moses) in the family, who was considered a bad character, to the surprise of the family, asked permission the week before to attend this meeting. As soon as the insurrection was reported, of course, this singular request was explained. But the report of their laying their plans at this church seemed to conflict with Nat's confession, unless this was another party which was to act in concert with him and failed to do so."[1] The whites were conducting a revival service at Barnes' on the 14th of August, and many negroes were present who had the privilege of worshiping with the whites and also of attending services conducted by preachers of their own color. Nat preached on this date, and seemed to have gained many sympathizers, who signified their willingness to co-operate with him by wearing around their necks red bandanna handkerchiefs, and who in many ways showed their rebellious spirit.[2] This behavior was not understood until after the insurrection.

The plot was also in contemplation for a greater time than is generally believed. As early as 1825 Nat Turner was preaching, and he astounded the slaves by his strange utterances and deeds. A letter from Jerusalem of Sep-

[1] Dr. W. H. Daughtry, Sunbeam, Virginia.
[2] They tried to ride over white people.

tember, 21, says that a negro woman belonging to Mr. Solomon Parker stated that she had heard the subject discussed among her master's slaves and those of the neighborhood eighteen months before the insurrection. For several years plans for insurrection were maturing in the mind of Nat Turner, and by February, 1831, he had so far determined upon his scheme that he related it to four of the most influential negroes of his section. From that time every effort was made to enlist the co-operation of other slaves, but with the greatest patience and prudence. The negro woman above mentioned said that in May and August she had heard several negroes express themselves as determined to unite against the whites, and that they had threatened to kill her if she told. The slaves of Mr. Benjamin Edwards testified that they had heard that "General Nat" was going to kill all the white people and that the negroes would be forced to join him or be killed. Berry Newsom, a free negro, on Monday, August 22d, remarked in the presence of these slaves that "the damn rascal" (Mr. Edwards) had been where they were at work, but that the negroes would get him before night.

The insurrection was a failure through no want of exertion on the part of the leaders, but on account of the refusal of the slaves in general to participate. This was due partially to fear. Many negroes besides those of Boykins District would have participated had the insurgents been more successful and less readily suppressed. The greatest restraint upon the slaves, however, was affection and good judgment. Their treatment and training had been such as to inspire obedience and contentment. Consequently, only sixty or seventy negroes were implicated, and of these only about forty were guilty, the remainder being forced to participate. Well might the Richmond Compiler of August 25th say: "The militia of Southamp-

THE SOUTHAMPTON INSURRECTION. 159

ton had been most active in ferreting out the fugitives from their hiding places, which was, of course, to be expected from their superior knowledge of their county. But it deserves to be said to the credit of many of the slaves whom gratitude had bound to their masters, that they had manifested the greatest alacrity in detecting and apprehending many of the brigands. They had brought in several, and a fine spirit had been shown in many of the plantations of confidence on the part of the masters and gratitude on the part of the slaves." In the same strain a letter from Norfolk to the National Gazette of August 24th says: "There is very little disaffection in the slaves generally, and they cannot muster a force sufficient to effect any object of importance. The few who have thus rushed headlong into the arena will be shot down like crows or captured and made examples of. The militia are collecting in all the neighboring counties and the utmost vigilance prevails." An express from Suffolk[1] says: "We have intimation that the insurrection was not the result of concert to any extent, nor rested on any combination to give the least chance of success. This is evident from the small number of adherents which the ringleaders, with all their threats and persuasions, were enabled to enlist in their cause. The slaves throughout the county are generally well affected and even faithful to their employers." While no estimate can be made of the damage that might have been done had these few fanatics been able to discipline their followers, the people of Wilmington, North Carolina, expressed the sentiment of the slave-holders of Virginia, as follows: "That the Nat Turner insurrection could not be dismissed without speaking of the good behavior of the slaves thereabouts, who might be entrusted, it was believed, to take part in the defense of the

[1] Norfolk Herald, August 26, 1831.

community under any circumstances." Thus it was that the insurrection only served to bind master and slave in tighter bonds of affection, so that upon the surrender at Appomattox both wept at the thought of separation.

RESULTS OF THE INSURRECTION.—The immediate result of the insurrection was the greatest excitement, alarm, and confusion in many parts of the South. Men went about in groups, the militia drills were renewed, and the arms, called in a few months before, reissued. Mr. Thomas Gray says: "The late insurrection in Southampton has greatly excited the public mind and led to a thousand idle, exaggerated, and mischievous reports. It is the first instance in our history of an open rebellion of the slaves, and attended with such atrocious circumstances of cruelty and destruction as could not fail to leave a deep impression, not only on the minds of the community where the fearful tragedy was wrought, but throughout every portion of our country in which this population is to be found." The least suspicion of another plot would have involved not only the guilty, but the innocent negroes, in indiscriminate murder. The Norfolk Herald in September said: "We were struck with the coincidence of opinion in the article from the Whig with the suggestion of our own mind before we saw that paper, and which we expressed in our last number, namely; that, judging from the excitement produced by the Southampton murders on the minds of the whites in that and adjacent counties, any future outrage of the blacks of a similar character would be retaliated by their indiscriminate destruction. The arm of law would be inadequate to protect even the innocent from the general flood of vengeance and extermination."

By December, 1831, all alarm had passed away and the people were in a position to consider carefully the actual status of the negro and what should be his future. The general public sentiment was in favor of emancipation,[1] and with this in view special pains had been taken to choose worthy and intelligent men for the Legislature, which was to meet in December. Howison[2] says of the result: "The next Legislature was one of intelligence and talent." A permanent organization having been formed, the first question which confronted the Legislature was the consideration of the various petitions concerning the future of slavery. The Governor foresaw the threatening evil, and said: "As a means of guarding against the possible repetition of these sanguinary scenes, I cannot fail to recommend to your early attention the revision of all the laws intended to preserve in due subordination the slave population of our State. In urging these considerations upon you, let me not be understood as expressing the slightest doubt or apprehension of general results. All communities are liable to suffer from the dagger of the murderous and midnight assassin, and it behooves them to guard against these. With us, the first returning light dispels the danger and soon witnesses the murderer in chains."

The insurrection caused no fear of a successful servile insurrection, nor did it create a spirit of hostility to the slaves, but it centered public consideration upon the following pertinent questions: Is not slavery the cause of the decline in the value of lands in certain portions of Virginia? Is it not the cause of emigration (directly or indirectly) from Virginia, and the lack of a dense white population? Is it not time to ask the Legislature to lessen the slave population, even with a view to final abolition?

[1] Mr. Montgomery says that many attributed the Nat Turner insurrection to the articles of William L. Garrison and others in the Liberator, but that this was not so, for Garrison never opposed slavery in higher terms than did leading Virginians of the Legislature of 1831 and 1832.—Student's History of the United States, p. 312.
[2] History of Virginia.

162   THE SOUTHAMPTON INSURRECTION.

Would it not be expedient to tax slaves so high as to lessen their value and apply the proceeds to, (1) the removal and colonization of such as their masters will give up, (2) removing free negroes, and (3) buying and colonizing the slaves, taking care to provide for the support of the State government by tax on other property? Would not such tax on slaves, by reducing their price, increase the Southern trade to an extent greatly beneficial to Virginia? Is it not advisable, that the Legislature of Virginia adopt measures to bring about the amendment to the Constitution of the United States, so as to allow Congress to appropriate money for transporting free negroes and for purchasing slaves and sending them to Africa? It was not the intention of the Legislature to discuss these questions with open doors. Consequently, a select committee was appointed to investigate all questions relating to slaves, free negroes, and mulattoes, and the Governor was requested to lay before it all the papers and documents relating to the Southampton massacre. But, unfortunately, Mr. Goode, of Mecklenburg, moved that the memorials for the gradual emancipation of the slaves and the removal of the free negroes and slaves from Virginia should not be submitted to the select committee. This was defeated by a vote of 93 to 27, after which he moved that this committee be discharged, as it was inexpedient to legislate on the subject. Mr. Randolph immediately moved that this motion be so amended as to instruct the committee 'to inquire into the expediency of submitting to the qualified voters of the several towns, cities, boroughs, and counties of the Commonwealth the propriety of providing by law that the children of all private slaves who may be born in the State on or after the 4th of July, 1840, shall become the property of the Commonwealth, the males at twenty-one years and the females at eighteen, if detained by their owners within the limits of Virginia until they shall have arrived at that age; and that they shall be hired out until the net sum arising therefrom shall be sufficient to defray the expense of their removal beyond the limits of the United States.' Mr. Randolph's motion was carried by a vote of 116 to 7, but Mr. Brodnax, chairman of the committee, reported as the opinion of the committee, "That it is inexpedient for the present to make any legislative enactment for the abolition of slavery." This report was adopted, and Mr. Bryce, of Goochland, moved to so amend the report as to prefix thereto the following: "Profoundly sensible of the great evils arising from the condition of the colored population of this Commonwealth; induced by humanity as well as by policy to an immediate effort for the removal, in the first place, as well of those who are now free, as of such as may hereafter become free; believing that this effort, while it is in just accordance with the sentiment of the community on the subject, will absorb all our present means; and that a further action for the removal of the slaves should await a more definite development of public opinion; Resolved," etc. This motion was carried, and the condition of the free negro was the next question in order.

They had been allowed most of the privileges of the whites, except the right of suffrage.[1] Freely marrying among the slaves, they had ready access to them, and had been actively employed in distributing inflammatory papers. Governor Floyd, consequently, recommended as indispensably necessary that the Legislature should, in the spirit of kindness which has ever characterized it, appro-

---

[1] The laws of Virginia have always been prudent as to the right of suffrage, only those being considered eligible voters who have an interest in the government. The acts of 1655 and 1670 permitted only freeholders and housekeepers to vote. Indented servants were considered dangerous, as liable to create disturbances at elections. (Hening Statutes, vol. I, pp. 405, 411, 475; Cook's History of Virginia, pp. 222-224.) The right of suffrage was not taken from the free negroes till 1762.

priate an annual sum of money for the removal of this people, as a last benefit, which the State was enabled to confer upon them. In accordance with this recommendation, the expediency of setting apart for this object so much of the claims of Virginia on the general government as might belong to, and come into, the treasury of the State was debated, and the following resolutions were passed: "Resolved, That the Senate cause to be laid before the House a copy of the correspondence between Governor Monroe and President Jefferson in 1801, and subsequently growing out of an act of the Assembly adopted at the preceding session, by which it was made the duty of the Governor to correspond with the President on the subject of the purchase of lands out of the State, to which persons obnoxious to the laws or dangerous to the peace of society may be removed, and also that the executive lay before the House such part of the correspondence as remained on file in that department." On the 3d of February a motion was made in the Virginia House that the Senate and House of Representatives empower the Governor to apply to the general government, in behalf of the General Assembly, to procure a territory or territories beyond the limits of the United States, to which the several States might remove the whole or any part of the colored population, and that the Senators and Representatives of the State in Congress be requested to use their efforts to promote that object. This motion was tabled to await the result of a bill introduced by Mr. Brodnax, of the select committee, which was introduced on the 28th of January. The latter bill, however, was indefinitely postponed by a vote of 18 to 14 in the Senate, and, consequently, the former was never taken up. Mr. Brodnax's bill was for the removal of free negroes, or such as should become free and were willing to be removed, to some place beyond the limits of the United States. It forbade coercion except as to the free negroes, who remained in the State contrary to

THE SOUTHAMPTON INSURRECTION. 165

the laws of 1806, and it appropriated $35,000 for 1832 and $90,000 for 1833 for transportation. The place of removal was left to the discretion of a central board, to consist of the Governor, Treasurer, and members of the Council of State, who should have power to appoint agencies in Norfolk, Portsmouth, and other places as they, upon the recommendation of the county and corporation courts, should see fit.

All plans for emancipation and colonization had come to naught. But why? Public sentiment was evidently in favor of emancipation.[1] To all candid students of history this is evident. The principal revenues of the State were derived from lands and slaves, and without the slaves there was no immediately available labor. Consequently, if the negroes were transported before other labor could

[1] A memorial to the Legislature by the ladies of Fluvanna county should be instanced. It says: "We cannot conceal from ourselves that an evil is among us, which threatens to outgrow the growth and eclipse the brightness of our national blessings. Our daughters and their daughters are destined to become, in their turn, the tender fosterers of helpless infancy, the directors of developing childhood, and the companions of those citizens, who will occupy the legislative and executive offices of their country. Can we calmly anticipate the condition of the Southern States at that period, should no remedy be devised to arrest the progressive miseries attendant on slavery? Will the absent father's heart be at peace, when, amid the hurry of public affairs, his truant thoughts return to the home of his affection, surrounded by doubtful, if not dangerous, subjects to precarious authority? Perhaps when deeply engaged in his legislative duties his heart may quail and his tongue falter with irresistible apprehension for the peace and safety of objects dearer than life.

"We can only aid the mighty task by ardent outpourings of the spirit of supplication at the Throne of Grace. We will call upon the God, in whom we trust, to direct your counsels by His unerring wisdom, guide you with His effectual spirit. We now conjure you by the sacred charities of kindred, by the solemn obligations of justice, by every consideration of domestic affection and patriotic duty, to nerve every faculty of your minds to the investigation of this important subject, and let not the united voices of your mothers, wives, daughters and kindred have sounded in vain in your ears."

be introduced the land would be left idle and the State in poverty. Besides, revenues were not sufficient to purchase the slaves, and at the same time bear the expense of transportation, and the people realized that such a body of persons, unprepared for citizenship, would be a greater evil than slavery itself, both to themselves and to the country at large.[1] Colonization on the American continent was deemed inexpedient on the same grounds. Mr. Samuel J. Mills, one of the original promoters of the American Board of Missions and the American Bible Society, who had made a special study of the negro, said, when a project was set on foot to colonize the blacks beyond the Ohio river: "Whether any of us live to see it or not, the time will come when the white men will want all that region, and will have it, and our colony would be overwhelmed."[2] Mr. Monroe said, in 1829: "As to the people of color, if the Southern States wished to emancipate them, they might invite the United States to assist them; but without such invitation the other States ought not and would not interfere." But the Legislature of 1831-32 had witnessed the evils of petitions and requests for and in regard to slavery, and concluded that such requests implied the right of the general government to emancipate the slaves, and so compromised the dignity and honor of Virginia. The sentiment in Virginia, how-

[1] "All must concur, however," says the committee of the United States Senate appointed on the subject of the colonization of the free people of color in 1827, "in regarding the present condition of the free colored race in America as inconsistent with its future social and political advancement, and, where slavery exists at all, as calculated to aggravate its evils without any atoning good." Continuing, the committee said: "Their own consciousness of their degraded condition in the United States, has appealed to the North as well as the South, in their repeated efforts to find a territory beyond the limits of the Union to which they may retire and on which, secure from external danger, they may hope for the enjoyment of political as well as civil liberty."

[2] Latimer, Europe in Africa in XIXth Century, p. 292.

THE SOUTHAMPTON INSURRECTION. 167

ever, had always been in favor of the colonization of the negro, and the first efforts in that direction had come from this State. The words of the Congressional committee of 1827 sufficiently show this. "Anterior to the year 1806," it says, "three several attempts to procure a country suited to this object had been secretly made by the General Assembly of Virginia, through a correspondence between the Executive of that State and the President of the United States. The last, but, at the same time, the earliest public effort to attain this object, was made by the Legislature of the same State in December, 1816, some time before the formation, in the city of Washington, of the American Society for Colonizing the Free People of Color. The design of this institution, the committee are apprised, originated in the disclosure of the secret resolutions of prior Legislatures of that State, to which may also be ascribed, it is understood, the renewal of their obvious purpose in the resolution subjoined to this report,[1] a resolution which was first adopted by the House of Delegates of Virginia on the 14th of December, 1816, with a unanimity which denoted the deep interest that it inspired, and which openly manifested to the world a steady adherence to the humane policy which had secretly animated the same councils at a much earlier period. This brief and correct history of the origin of the American Colonization Society evinces that it sprang from a deep solicitude for Southern interests, and among those most competent to discern and to promote them." This sentiment remained unchanged after 1831.

Secondly, any free discussion or legislation in regard to slavery tended to arouse the slaves and create the opinion that the South was alarmed, notwithstanding the fact that the Southampton tragedy convinced slave-hold-

[1]This resolution is to the House of Representatives, asking aid in suppressing the slave trade and in colonizing the free people of color.

168 THE SOUTHAMPTON INSURRECTION.

ers that a servile insurrection was henceforth impossible. In 1829 the negroes of Eastern Virginia had contemplated freeing themselves if the Constitutional Convention of that year failed to emancipate them. Hence it was that the Legislature referred all such questions to a select committee.[1] Mr. Roan, a most earnest advocate of emancipation, exclaimed, when the matter had been unexpectedly introduced: "I think and feel, sir, that this subject has been most prematurely and injudiciously thrust upon the consideration of the House." Consequently, public sentiment, which was daily growing in favor of abolition, not having been sufficiently canvassed, the Legislature deemed it advisable to postpone all consideration of emancipation and colonization to a more appropriate occasion.

Three-fourths of the session of the Legislature had been spent in fruitless discussion of emancipation and colonization. Still, these discussions helped to allay the fears of the people and convinced them that a strict enforcement of existing laws, which, from a too strong sense of security, had not been insisted upon before, was more necessary than new legislation. Mr. Gray writes: "It (the insurrection) is calculated also to demonstrate the policy of our laws in restraint of that class of our population, and induce all those entrusted with their execution, as well as our citizens generally, to see that they are strictly and rigidly enforced. Each particular community should look to its own safety, whilst the general guardians of the laws keep a watchful eye over all." Consequently, a bill "To amend an act entitled an act to reduce into one the several acts concerning slaves, free negroes, and mulattoes, and for other purposes" was proposed and passed in order to render more accessible the laws on

[1] Secret discussion was legitimate and justified by the Constitution of the United States, Article I, Section 5, Clause 3.

THE SOUTHAMPTON INSURRECTION. 169

slavery, as well as to add thereto the following new enactments. The bill provided that slaves and free negroes should not thereafter conduct religious services, nor could they attend meetings held at night by white preachers, unless with the written permission of master or overseer.[1] It further provided that "No free negro or mulatto shall hereafter be capable of purchasing or otherwise acquiring permanent ownership, except by descent, to any slave other than his or her husband, wife or children," and prescribed very rigid punishment for persons writing or printing anything advising persons of color to rebel.[2] These enactments were not more stringent than measures adopted by preceding Legislatures. The Legislature of 1830 and 1831 prohibited the instruction of mulattoes, free negroes, and slaves.[3] Henceforth there was a more guarded public, but the Legislature of 1831-32 was one of wisdom and moderation. Petitions were presented that slaves and free negroes be forbidden to own hogs, dogs, and other property, and that they be denied the privilege of becoming millers, mechanics, tradesmen, etc. These requests were rejected as being unnecessary and unbecoming. The law providing for burning in the hand was

[1] This act did not interfere with religious meetings on the farm of the owner of the slaves. Slaves could also attend meetings in company with their owners, and without them, provided they had a written permission. Also certain worthy negroes continued to preach and conduct meetings. "Uncle Jack," of Amelia county, who, when a child, had been kidnaped in Africa and landed on James River from the last slave ship that landed its cargo in Virginia, held public meetings for negroes. Howe, History of Virginia, p. 174. At the present time the natives of South Africa are required to have passes, in default of which they may be detained on their journey.

[2] Such laws had been passed by other States previous to 1831. Hurd, Freedom and Bondage, vol. II, p. 105. Not even Nat's confession to Mr. Gray could be sold in the South.

[3] This did not apply to the gratuitous instruction of slaves by masters, nor did it prevent the private instruction of free blacks by other persons. Hurd, Ibid, vol. II.

170   THE SOUTHAMPTON INSURRECTION.

repealed, but a request for the repeal of the act providing for the payment of a condemned slave was refused on the ground that it was often a security for the just and impartial trial of slaves. In all the slave States the same moderation was followed. This was partially due to the desire of avoiding all suspicion of action that might be used by the abolitionists as an argument for immediate emancipation. There was some further restrictive legislation, however. Thus Mr. Brackett says: "The (Maryland) act of 1806, mild in its provisions and milder still in its results, might have remained long on the statute books had not the work of Nat Turner and his handful of followers in Virginia cast suspicion over the movements of the blacks far and wide."[1] Many of the Southern States held Constitutional Conventions after 1831, and the free negroes, who previously had been allowed the right of suffrage, were deprived of it.[2] In the same spirit, the uni-

[1] The Negro in Maryland, p. 199.
[2] Moore, History of North Carolina, vol. II, pp. 30-34. Mr. Moore says of the North Carolina Convention of 1835 and of the state of affairs then existing: "The relations between the two races constituting the population of North Carolina at the period to which reference is made were most unhappy and deplorable. The insurrection in the neighboring county of Southampton, in the State of Virginia, produced a lasting train of disagreeable and unfortunate consequences. * * * Jealousy and distrust took possession of the Southern white people. An increasing fear and indiscriminate resentment disgraced localities far removed from and utterly unconnected with the scene of disturbance. Nat Turner's misdeeds silenced a thousand able orators, and, for many years, robbed African religious observances of much of their previous freedom and uproar. * * * Under the Constitution of 1776 the free negroes of North Carolina had been permitted to vote. There was no provision in the original law which explicitly gave them this privilege, but after the Revolution they by degrees acquired the habit of voting. The best and most enlightened men of both parties vainly endeavored to continue the franchise to such as should possess a small freehold qualification; but this was rejected. The growing sectional feeling between the North and the South deafened the ears and steeled the hearts of our people too often, when justice and mercy were indicating larger privilege and protection to the unhappy free blacks."

versal opinion of the old slave is: "We would have been better off if the insurrection had never occurred." The most stringent legislation against the introduction of negroes and the circulation of incendiary publications was resorted to. But, on the whole, the words of Mr. Floyd may be applied to the period from 1831 to 1865, that, "These (negro preachers) our laws have heretofore treated with indulgent kindness, and many instances of solicitude for the negroes have marked the progress of legislation."

Previous to 1831 colonization societies had been active, not only in transporting free negroes, but also in inducing masters to free their slaves. In 1829 Mr. Monroe said: "The American Colonization Society has, at all times, solemnly disavowed any purpose of interfering with the institutions or rights of our Southern communities. By the soundest and most judicious minds of our country it has, however, been regarded as developing and demonstrating the practicableness and utility of a plan which commends itself as worthy of adoption to those individuals and States who desire not only to benefit the free people of color, while they relieve themselves by their removal, but also to diminish and finally eradicate what all sober and unprejudiced minds regard as the greatest of our national evils, the system of slavery." These societies disappeared from the North, anti-slavery societies taking their place, and in the South their principles were changed, by the increase of abolition literature, now supported by an abolition press, issuing the Liberator, the African Sentinel and the Genius of Universal Emancipation. Dr. Brock says: "Through the discord produced by these incendiaries nearly three years elapsed before the Colonization Society of Virginia had another meeting." But the South was the more resolved upon transportation, though its efforts were confined to the removal of the free people of color and not of slaves. At a meeting in

January, 1832, the Virginia Colonization Society "Resolved, That this society deems it expedient at this time to renew its pledges to the public strictly to adhere to the original feature in the constitution, which confines its operations to the removal of the free people of color only with their consent." The Junior Colonization Society induced the General Assembly in 1833 to appropriate $18,000 annually for five years for the removal of free blacks to Liberia. In 1850, on the recommendation of Mr. Floyd, President of the Virginia Colonization Society, $30,000 per annum for five years were appropriated for this purpose, and in 1853 a colonization board was established and the above amount continued for five years.[1] The Virginia Colonization Society colonized from one to two hundred negroes per year until the outbreak of the War of 1861. The Richmond Whig, commenting upon the hostility of the abolitionists to the colonization societies, said: "Another revolution of public sentiment almost as remarkable and much more intelligible has occurred in the South in respect to the African colonization. The original opponents in that quarter of the Union have generally grounded their arms. This opposition has been subdued by reason and experience. They have seen success crown the undertaking. They behold the great good it is effecting to both races, and they have been convinced and converted. It is for that reason that the fanatics have thrown themselves against it. In expended, progressive, and permanent benefit to the human race we believe it the master scheme of this or any other age." Thus very appropriately might ex-Governor Wise say, in 1840: "Africa gave to Virginia a savage and a slave; Virginia gives back to Africa a citizen and a Christian."

[1] Private persons freed their negroes and made provision for their removal to Liberia. Also private contributions were made to the Colonization Society. Southampton aided 200 negroes to emigrate in 1831. John Randolph, of Roanoke, freed his slaves in 1833 and bequeathed $30,000 for their transportation to Ohio.

THE SOUTHAMPTON INSURRECTION. 173

In the North the immediate effect of the insurrection was a state of affairs similar to that in the South, a more pronounced conviction of the evils of slavery. But the South had to adapt herself to existing circumstances, while in the North a spirit of imagined philanthropy endeavored to force the South to the immediate abolition of slavery. There existed an honest conviction that the South was opposed to emancipation, and that the Southampton massacre was the result of the harsh treatment of the slaves. William Lloyd Garrison, commenting on the Governor's proclamation for the arrest of Nat Turner, said: "How wonder at his determined efforts to avenge his wrongs, when he had a scar on his temple, also one on the back of his neck, and a large knot on one of the bones of his right arm near the wrist, produced by blows?"[1] These misrepresentations had the desired effect in the North, but in the South it was the opposite. Mr. Howison says: "The idea of general emancipation had many supporters, and nothing but the sinister influences from abroad prevented its triumph." So Mr. Alexander writes:[2] "Alarm and indignation spread throughout the Southern country like an electric spark. The effect on the people of the South in regard to slavery was the very opposite of that aimed at; sentiments more favorable to the continuance and even perpetuity of slavery began now to be commonly entertained, whereas before such sentiments were scarcely ever heard."[3] "From the year

[1] Nat confessed to the kind treatment of his master. The scar on his neck was produced by a bite from one of his companions, the one on his temple from a mule kick, and the knot on his arm was due to another fray with a negro.—Richmond Enquirer, October 25, 1831.

[2] African Colonization, p. 383.

[3] Negroes had been introduced into Virginia against her wishes. O'Callaghan says: "To the Dutch undoubtedly belongs the questionable distinction of having first introduced negro slaves into the colonies, now the United States of America." If by "slaves" negro servants are meant, this is true. Even Williams, the negro

1776," says Dr. Brock, "the prevalent opinion in Virginia was that slavery was not entailed on the State forever. Until 1831 (the date of the rise of the bitter abolition crusade) none of her economists, with the exception of William B. Giles, had defended it as an abstract right. The opinion of Washington, Mason, Jefferson, Monroe, Marshall, the Randolphs, and, indeed, of all of her leading statesmen of the era are well known and had been frequently expressed. Schemes of general emancipation of the slaves of Virginia were proposed to the Legislature by Jefferson in 1776, by William Craighead, Dr. William Thornton in 1785, St. George Tucker in 1796, Thomas Jefferson Randolph in 1832, and by others." Now, however, he thinks "Sentiments more favorable to the perpetuity of slavery began now to be commonly entertained."[1]

The Southampton massacre increased the number of

historian, by no means the apologist of Virginians, concedes that "It is due to the Virginia Colony to say that the slaves were forced upon them; that white servitude was common." Far from being an advocate of slavery, she furnished "the first man who ever lifted up his voice against the African slave trade," Rev. Morgan Godwin, a minister of the Church of England in Virginia during the administration of Governor Berkley. He afterward went from Virginia to the Barbadoes, where "he fought a good fight for the negro and the Indian in the face of fierce opposition." Ballagh, Conservative Review, August, 1899, "Institutional Origin of Slavery." O'Callaghan, Voyages of the Slaves; Introduction, pp. 6-8. George W. Williams, History of the Negro Race in America. Slaughter's Colonial Church of Virginia, p. 40. Clarkson, History of the Abolition of the Slave Trade, vol. I, p. 46.

[1] But this must not be taken in the extreme sense. It was a sentiment in favor of the perpetuity of slavery rather than of being forced to submit to the evils of the "petting" system of the extreme sentimentalists, by which the inferior race was spoiled and delayed in their progress toward civilization. The evils of this system have been too well illustrated in more recent troubles in Zululand, South Africa. Mr. Knox Little, Canon of Worcester, England, says: "Besides the mischievous influences of Bishop Colenso on the church of South Africa, his sentimental and absurd views as to the Zulus did great harm and are crucial examples of this kind of tone." South Africa, p. 294.

fanatics, and, together with the British statute which set free 800,000 negroes within a few miles of our Atlantic coast, produced the most profound impression upon the citizens of all sections of the country. This was the second great body of negroes which had been freed within sight of the southern shores of the United States. The abolitionists immediately sent agents to England to import more orators and to further arouse the British officials near the coasts of the United States. The Legislatures of several of the Southern States were assembled several months before the usual time to take measures against these dangers, and to prevent the introduction of vicious negroes from other States.[1] Southern towns instituted the custom of ringing "curfew" at nine o'clock in the evening, after which no negro was allowed abroad without a pass, and this custom was continued until the war between the States. Fifteen years later a distinguished English traveler wrote: "Every evening at nine o'clock a great bell, or curfew, tolls in the market-place of Montgomery, after which no colored man is permitted to be abroad without a pass. This custom has, I understand, continued ever since some formidable insurrections which happened several years ago in Virginia and elsewhere."[2] In October, 1833, Judge A. P. Upshur, of Northampton county, afterward Secretary of State of the United States, wrote to the Governor: "Indeed, the protection uniformly afforded by individuals and private societies in the North to fugitive slaves from the South is too notorious to be denied, and presents, as it seems to me, a fit occasion for the interference of the aggrieved States. It is perfectly certain that unless this abuse can, in some mode or other, be speedily corrected, the eastern shore of Virginia, affording as it does, and must continue to do by its very posi-

[1] Niles Register, December 1, 1831.
[2] Lyell's Travels in the United States, vol. ii, p. 43.

tion, every facility for the escape of slaves, will soon be wholly without that species of property. The impoverishment and ruin of the people will be the necessary consequences. It is obvious that the exertions of the individual owners can effect very little in reclaiming these slaves from communities organized against their rights. Hence, almost every attempt of that kind has not only failed of success, but has subjected the party to public insult and personal danger. Their best hope, and, indeed, their only hope, must be found in the interference of the public authorities of our States." In September of the following year a suspicious character made his appearance at Fairfax Court House. He told the negroes that he had persuaded the negroes of Prince William and other counties to make an effort for freedom, saying openly: "If you will only be true you can get free." Several negroes were arrested and examined. Thy stated that he gave them money, and told them that he had plenty of arms and ammunition. This white fanatic became alarmed and fled to Alexandria. He told the negroes and a white woman, however, that he would return in two weeks, and appointed a place two miles from the courthouse at which they were to assemble.

These agents increased, became more daring, and flooded the country with inflammatory and incendiary publications. In 1835, at Charleston, the postoffice was so flooded with such papers that the people forced the postmaster to destroy them. In response to the latter's appeal for orders, the Postmaster General replied: "By no act or direction of mine, official or private, could I be induced to aid knowingly in giving circulation to papers of this description, directly or indirectly." And he further said that he would not sanction and would not condemn the course the postmaster had taken in refusing to deliver certain mail matter. Likewise, in Richmond, Virginia, and in other places, the people invoked the aid of the Postmaster General to such an extent that President Jackson's

THE SOUTHAMPTON INSURRECTION. 177

message of 1835 protested against the abolition societies, and recommended that Congress forbid the carrying by the United States mails of documents calculated to arouse the evil passions of the slaves and to produce insurrection among them.[1] The following letter will indicate the strength of the abolition and British influence upon the negroes in 1840. Mr. John E. Page, of Clarke county, Virginia, wrote to the Governor: "You have, as I have been informed, received from my brother, Dr. Page, of North Carolina, a narrative of an outrage recently committed upon a party, of whom I was one, at Chippewa, Canada, by a company of negro troops in the British service and wearing British uniforms. It is proper that I should corroborate the statement referred to and adopt it as my own, and, as a citizen of Virginia, request any action on the part of Your Excellency which in your judgment shall seem proper. While Englishmen travel by thousands through Virginia, and are received with a courtesy faulty only in its excess, citizens of Virginia and of the South cannot go to Canada without meeting at its very threshold outrages from an armed band of negroes, who are doubtless for the most part fugitives from the Southern States, and whose very organization as a British corps is an

[1] It was in the same year that several members of Congress took measures to destroy the anti-slavery societies in order that the mistaken philanthropists might be separated from the reckless fanatic and the incendiary, and an end be put to publications and petitions which, whatever their design, would have no other effect than to impede the object which they invoked and to aggravate the evil which they deplored. Pictures of slave degradation and misery, and of the white man's luxury and cruelty were exhibited. It is well to note one of these pictures sent Mr. Benton in 1835. It was an engraving representing a large, spreading tree of liberty, beneath whose shade a slave owner was at one time luxuriously reposing, with slaves fanning him; at another, carried forth in a palanquin to view the half-naked laborers in the cotton field, whom drivers, with whips, were scourging to their task. Benton. Thirty Years in the United States Senate, vol. I, p. 377.

insult to our Southern institutions." The state of affairs grew worse. In 1845 the Governor of Ohio threatened to invade Virginia to release a prisoner captured in the very act of inducing slaves to flee from their masters. The Southern people felt that these evils must be remedied, and for this purpose the Governor of Virginia, in 1856, wrote to the Governors of the Southern States: "Events are approaching which address themselves to your responsibilities and to mine as chief executives of the slave-holding States. Contingencies may soon happen which would require preparation for the worst of evils to the people we govern. Ought we not to admonish ourselves by joint counsel of the extraordinary duties which may devolve upon us from the dangers which so palpably threaten our common peace and safety? I propose that as early as convenient the Governors of Maryland, Virginia, etc., shall assemble at Raleigh, N. C., for the purpose generally of consultation upon the state of the country, upon the best means of preserving its peace, and especially of protecting the honor and interests of the slaveholding States."

As peddlers, booksellers, etc., abolitionists traversed all Virginia during the years preceding the war between the States, and, though mere agents, were received with much hospitality. John E. Cook, the brother-in-law of Governor Willard, of Indiana, and one of the principal lieutenants of John Brown, was especially active as a book agent. He is said to have visited Southampton, and in the early autumn of 1858 he went to the home of Dr. Thomas Maddox, in the Tilghmanton district, of Washington county, and sold a copy of Headley's "Life of Washington." He said his name was S. Stearns, and asked to stay all night, which request was cheerfully complied with. At supper he asked an inordinately long "grace," and after the meal disappeared for several hours. It was afterward learned that he had been in the kitchen urging the slaves to kill their master to gain their freedom, but the proposition was resented with horror by the slaves. So great was the strength of the abolition movement in 1860 that even the Northern Methodists and other religious sects in Virginia held secret meetings with the negroes in attempts to incite them to rebellion. Rev. E. D. Neill, the historian, was teaching on the eastern shore of Virginia and fled in fear of being tarred and feathered for attending such meetings.[1]

After 1831 the public was very sensitive to the least suspicion of servile revolt. Every August the alarm was given and the people rushed headlong to the swamps, the negroes as well as the whites, each household trusting the fidelity of its own, but suspecting that of the other slaves of the neighborhood. In December, 1856, the people of Fauquier, King and Queen, Culpeper and Rappahannock counties, and Lynchburg, Gordonsville and Petersburg were aroused by the report that the negroes were in a state of rebellion. Such reports were frequent and kept the people constantly on the alert. The John Brown raid, in 1859, encouraged by external aid and sympathy, proves how well grounded was this suspicion. It was believed that the raid was a general insurrection of the negroes, headed by 250 abolitionists, and the number of the raiders was not known until they were captured. The ready response of the State militia, however, and the loyalty of the slaves on this occasion and

[1] Probably this accounts for his hostility to Virginia in his History of the London Company. He afterwards became secretary to President Lincoln and later still a foreign Minister. These speeches and pictures appealed not to the understanding of the slaves, but to their passions; inspired vague hopes and stimulated abortive and fatal insurrections, since they could only understand the anti-slavery societies as allies, organized for action and ready to march to their aid on the first sign of insurrection.

throughout the war between the States demonstrate the efficiency of the slave legislation necessitated by the insurrection of 1831. But the insurrection is still remembered, and reports even now of an intended "rising" of the negroes are not uncommon.[1]

[1] In 1890 a letter from one negro to another detailing a well-planned plot was found in Franklin, Southampton county. Troops from Suffolk, Portsmouth and Norfolk held themselves in readiness to march at the first notification from telegraph operators, who remained at their posts the entire night.

CHAPTER IV.

CONCLUSION.

The Southampton insurrection was a landmark in the history of slavery. Little was known of it on account of the suppression by the Southern States of all such reports as were likely to arouse an insurrectionary spirit and because of exaggerated accounts given in the North.[1] It was the forerunner of the great slavery debates which resulted in the abolition of slavery in the United States, and was, indirectly, most instrumental in bringing about this result. Its importance is truly conceived by the old negroes of Southampton and vicinity, who reckon all time from "Nat's Fray," or "Old Nat's War."[2] It is, in fact, the only plot by rebellious Southern negroes which deserves the name of insurrection. More negroes were connected with the Gabriel insurrection, but they were discovered, dispersed, and their leader executed without the loss of one white person. Both were influenced by the attempts of former insurgent slaves, but the Southampton rebellion was directly encouraged by the abolition movement in the United States, while Gabriel met with encouragement only from foreigners. The two insurrections also agree in that, in both, religious fanaticism and

---

[1]Some years since a Philadelphia paper stated that General George H. Thomas when a friendless, ragged and homeless boy was taken by Nat Turner to Washington and procured a commission to West Point. The General's sister, Miss Judith, replied: "Your statement is a lie. General Thomas had many friends, a comfortable home and a native State until he deserted them."

[2]Thomas Nelson Page tells of a fox which was noted for his shrewdness in avoiding the hunters. In consequence of this he was called "Nat Turner." Social Life in Virginia, p. 70.

delusion played a very important role. The true character of the negro and the nature of the institution of slavery in the American colonies and States can best be learned from a thorough study of slave revolts.

It continues a mystery why so few slave revolts occurred in the United States. Mr. Alexander Johnson says the reason could not have been due to the gentleness of the slave system, as it was increasing in its oppressions, nor to the affection of the slave for the master, nor the cowardice of the negro, as there have been cases when the negroes have proved themselves as brave as any people; but he insists that it is because "the race, by long contact with the white race, has imbibed something of that respect for law which has always characterized the latter, so that the negroes, however enterprising, when backed by the forms of law, patiently submitted to legal servitude."[1] This statement is contradictory and inconsistent with known facts. The first recorded instance of a negro rebellion in the United States took place in Massachusetts, where, if anywhere, law and order should have been effective, and the instances of insubordination among the negroes before 1865 were, in proportion to the population of blacks in the two sections, far more numerous in the free than in the slave States. In September of the year of the Southampton insurrection a serious race war occurred in Providence, Rhode Island. Begun by a row between seven white men and a few negroes, it continued for four consecutive days, and was not suppressed until three companies of infantry, one of cavalry, and one of artillery, besides the cadets of the town, had been called out. The Southampton insurrection is the only recorded instance in the South of a servile insurrection deserving the name. Including individual cases of the murder of a master or mistress, not more than one hundred people in

[1] Lalor's Encyclopedia, "Slave Insurrections."

Virginia suffered death at the hands of rebellious slaves. The instances of negro riots have been more frequent and more successful since than before 1865, as is too well shown by the negro riots of Darien, Georgia, and by recent outrages in other Southern States, as well as in the Western State of Illinois. The hostile spirit of the Butler Zouaves, who threatened to visit Warrenton in spite of the opposition of the Mayor of the town and the Governor of the State, illustrates the present feeling of numbers of the young blacks. The Richmond Dispatch of September 20, 1899, says: "The patience of the Southern people has been sorely tried for a year or two past, and there is no telling what extreme measures may have to be resorted to unless a better condition is brought about." Nor are these signs more evident in the South than in the North. On the other hand, the white race is becoming more law-abiding. In spite of the Mafia riot of New Orleans and others of more recent date, there are no upheavals of whites to be compared to Bacon's rebellion, the rebellion of the indented servants of Virginia in 1663, Dorr's, Shays', the Whisky rebellion, or the revolt along the Chesapeake and Ohio canal in 1838, all of which occurred in the palmiest days of slavery. Still there were few signs of discontent among the negroes. The explanation is that the blacks as slaves were improved in station and opportunities of life. They were not only civilized and Christianized, but they were taught manual labor, as well as given a plain, practical education, now important in the solution of the race problem in the United States, together with colonization. Booker Washington, the most intelligent representative of his race, recognizes this fact. Mr. James Bryce, the historian, says of the negroes of South Africa: "Manual education and the habit of steady industry are quite as much needed as book education, a conclusion at which the friends of the American negro have arrived."[1] Nor were the slaves addicted to passion, pillage, and theft as the modern negroes of America are. The negroes of Africa are said to be free from these as natural inclinations. This would seem to indicate that the negro, enjoying equal political rights with a superior race, is worse than in his native state. They realized their inferiority and were ready to learn, and were conscious of a desire on the part of the masters to supply their every want.[2] The masters were lenient, and only became more rigid when external forces rendered it necessary. Thus there sprang up a devotion between master and slave which increased from year to year. And after the war of secession Gen. J. B. Gordon wrote: "History records no instance of such disinterested loyalty. Though they had heard of the proclamation of their freedom, yet they protected and supported these defenseless women and children and committed no outrage."[3] This was the case, notwithstanding the fact that

[1] It is the general consensus of opinion that the negro carpenters, mechanics, etc., trained in slavery are more skilled than those who have acquired their trades since 1865. This is partly due to the fact that the negro of today, being self-dependent, cannot afford to spend a sufficient time at apprenticeship.

[2] "Had the African been left like the Indian, in his native freedom, his would have been the fate of the Indian. But in the mysterious Providence of God the African was 'bound to the care of the Anglo-American,' who has borne him along with him in his upward career, protecting his weakness and providing for his wants. Accordingly he has grown with our growth and strengthened with our strength, until he is numbered by millions instead of scores. In the mean time the black man has been trained in the habits, manners and acts of civilized life, been taught the Christian religion and been gradually rising in the intellectual and moral order, until he is far above his race in their native seats. In these facts we see traces of an all-wise Providence in permitting the black man to be brought here and subjected to the discipline of slavery tempered by Christianity and regulated by law. Verily, if there had been no other end of such a procedure, the seeming sharp Providence of God would have been highly justified." Slaughter's Virginia History of African Colonization, p 4.

[3] Report of Committee of Congress on Outrages, vol. VI, p. 334.

THE SOUTHAMPTON INSURRECTION. 185

news traveled among the slaves rapidly and mysteriously. Mrs. Latimer says of Stanley's trip through Africa: "Information seemed to travel among the natives rapidly and mysteriously, as it used to do during our Civil War among the negroes."[1] Such was the contentment of all classes of negroes then that free negroes as well as slaves offered their services as soldiers in the Confederate army.[2] And Southern statesmen were considering the question of employing them when the war was hastened to a close. The slaves were employed in minor capacities. They acted as spies, built fortifications, and cared for the comfort of their masters, yet few fled to the Federal army.[3] A company, organized from the employees of Winder Hospital, near Richmond, in the winter of 1864-65, acquired some proficiency in drill and appeared to be impressed with the common sentiment of their masters.[4]

Fear and want of organization, it is true, acted as a great restraint against servile insurrections. But this does not argue that the negro, under all circumstances, is a coward. Inspired by motives of love and affection, he is brave. In the Southampton insurrection the deeds of bravery of the slaves exceeded those of cowardice, but invariably those deeds were in defense of the helpless whites against the cowardice of their own race. Truthfully does Mr. Johnson say that the slave was inspired with a respect for law, but this respect was the result, not merely of long contact with the white race, but of the lessons of love, obedience, and confidence learned from kind, lenient, but positive masters. Considering these facts the most natu-

[1] Europe in Africa in the XIXth Century, p. 161.
[2] Governors' Letters.
[3] Fifteen or twenty slaves fled to Jamestown Island, and murdered three white men. But they were not organized and had no insurrectionary motives. They remained a few days in feasting and then fled to the Federal army at Williamsburg.
[4] Brock, Virginia Historical Collections, vol. VI.

186 THE SOUTHAMPTON INSURRECTION.

ral conclusion is that the North American institution of slavery produced a more obedient and law-abiding citizen than the modern free negro seems to be.

The emancipation of the slaves in 1865 was not a result of fear of servile insurrection nor of unanimity of Northern sentiment favoring it.[1] Servile insurrection tended to delay rather than quicken emancipation. The causes of the war between the States were far different from those generally assigned for it. The North and South were essentially on the same platform in regard to whether States might withdraw from the Union and whether the slaves should be emancipated. In the North as well as in the South there was a widespread conviction that the coercion of a State into the Union and the abolition of slavery by the Federal Government were violations of the Federal Constitution. At the outset the President, Congress, and the Supreme Court disavowed all such intentions, and the beginning of the war would have been doubtful had a different purpose been evinced. In Cincinnati, in Chicago, in Boston, and elsewhere demonstrations unfavorable to the Administration at Washington were put down before coming to a head.[2] Dr. Charles L. C. Minor says: "When a delegation urged Mr. Lincoln to emancipate the negroes by proclamation, he expressed the apprehension that if he should do as they wished fifty thousand rifles from the border States, then serving in the army of the Union, might go over to the opposing side. In McClure's Magazine for May, 1899, Miss Tarbell tells us that Mr. Lincoln said that if he should enlist negroes in his army, two hundred thousand muskets that he had put into the hands of the border States men would be turned against the Union army. There was actual danger of revolt in the army against the emancipation proclama-

[1] Johnson, A Short History of the War of Secession, pp. 11, 20.
[2] Marshall, American Bastile, p. 606, etc.

tion when Burnside turned over his army to Hooker." General Rosecrans reported to Washington the existence in the West of secret orders of men bound by oath to co-operate with the Confederates to the number of four hundred thousand men.[1] So in New York city the people defied the Federal Government for six days and stopped the drafting of soldiers until veterans from the Army of the Potomac interfered. Gorham, the latest biographer of Secretary Stanton, says that had Gettysburg resulted differently New York would have made no submission. In spite of this defeat of the Confederates, however, there was further resistance in New York to Federal authority. As late as June, 1864, Mr. Lincoln's emancipation proclamation failed to get in Congress the necessary two-thirds vote, and had to go over to the next session, when the war was practically over. In August of the same year Mr. Lincoln wrote to a friend a letter, in which he made several proposals for peace, but failed to mention slavery.[2] The Democratic candidate for President in 1864, General McClellan, received 81 per cent. of the votes of Mr. Lincoln,[3] notwithstanding the fact that soldiers were on duty at the polls,[4] and that, by order of the War Department, criticism of the Administration had been made treason, triable by court-martial.[5] The English Minister threatened interference by England on account of the formidable opposition manifested to the war in the Northern

[1] Nicolay and Hay, in "Life of Lincoln," mention this organization, but say 350,000 was an exaggeration of this number.

[2] This letter was never sent.

[3] This fact was collected by Provost R. P. Uhler, of the Peabody Library, from Edward Stanwood, who gathered it from "McPherson's Political Handbook." McPherson was Clerk of the House of Representatives when the official count was verified in the joint session of Congress.

[4] Stanwood's History of the Presidency, p. 304.

[5] Stanwood's History of the Presidency, p. 304. Marshall's American Bastile, pp. 5-11, etc.; 717-728.

States, but Mr. Seward replied: "By touching this little bell I can imprison a man in Maine. By touching it again I can imprison a man in California." President Andrews, of Brown University, as well as other distinguished Northern historians, concedes that abolition was opposed by an overwhelming majority of the Northern people, not only before, but during the entire war, and as long as opposition to it was safe.[1]

Likewise, there was a strong sentiment in the South in favor of abolition and opposed to secession. Dr. J. M. Callahan says: "In Virginia especially we see a strong sentiment in favor of emancipation." Though it is not true, as stated by General Wheeler, that as many men went from the South into the Northern armies as into the Southern, yet many leading Southerners, as Gen. George H. Thomas, did, and many others took up arms against the Union only when President Lincoln made the mistake of his life in calling for volunteers.[2] They believed coercion a violation of the Constitution and secession an unwise step, but preferred the latter to the former. Various plans were proposed by Confederate statesmen for the emancipation of the slaves and their enlistment in the army, and the foreign Ministers were instructed to recommend emancipation if necessary. As in the war with Spain the annexation of the Philippines was not the end originally contemplated, so in the war of 1861 emancipation was a war measure and not the result of a general conviction of the evils of slavery or of slave insurrection,

---

[1] I am much indebted to Dr. C. L. C. Minor for suggestions on this paragraph. His article, "Hopeless from the Beginning," published in the Norfolk Landmark of September 10, 1899, is excellent on this subject.

[2] It is doubtful if North Carolina and Virginia would have seceded if he had not made this call. In this case secession would have been only temporary separation, and on the return of the seceding States a more centralized government, as at present, would probably have been the result.

though John Brown's raid took place only a few years previous to this event.

History records no instance in which two races equally free have lived together in harmony. The Anglo-Boer dispute in the Transvaal is a question of race supremacy, and Sir Alfred Milner, the British Commissioner in South Africa, says: "It seems a paradox, but it is true that the only effective way of protecting our subjects is to help them to cease to be our subjects." Mr. Jefferson said that the negro and white races, equally free, could not live under the same government. They cannot amalgamate and solve the question as did Greece and Rome. Consequently, either the negro must be colonized or occupy an inferior position.[1] But that the negroes may occupy an inferior position in the United States, they must be equally distributed in all sections of the country. Otherwise in those sections farthest removed there will exist sympathy for the negro, and a misconception and misrepresentation of the relation of the two races. The whites of the North and West believe the negro is cheated

[1] The relation of the whites and blacks of South Africa serves as an illustration of the only condition under which an inferior and a superior race can live peacefully together. The blacks are a necessary part of the economic machinery of the country for mining, manufacturing, tillage or ranching. They perform the menial services, and are allowed many privileges. Many of them have amassed fortunes, and all enjoy equal religious privileges with the whites. But politically and socially the negro is the inferior of the white man. He has never held political rights in the Dutch Republics. The Dutch would scout such an idea and even reproach the English of Cape Colony with being "governed by black men." Among the other nations both property and educational requirements are necessary for the right of suffrage, which requirements are abused to defraud the negro equally as much as in the Southern States of America. Khama, a Christian African chief, was entertained in England by the Duke of Westminster and others. This greatly excited the indignation of the white population of South Africa. The native Africans recognize their inferiority, and consequently the two races live in harmony. Never has the negro been considered socially and politically equal by any race among whom he dwelt.

190 THE SOUTHAMPTON INSURRECTION.

and persecuted. In many sections it is actually believed that rejected lovers in the South black themselves and commit the outrages so frequently perpetrated by negroes. So far the two races have lived in the South as equals before the law, because the majority of the negroes remain conscious of the superiority of the white race. For this reason negro labor has been preferred to white. The negro gladly accepts gifts in the form of food, old clothes, etc, and performs menial services, as cook, coachman, and servant of every description. Custom and habit exclude the poor whites of the South from such offices. In this way the negroes are rapidly acquiring property which, together with the free schools, supported principally by the whites, free amusement, and cheap newspapers, enables them to give their children educations equal to that of the ordinary whites, while the poorer whites are unable to secure even common-school education. Consequently, the number of servants in the South is gradually decreasing, and the white people learning to perform for themselves the ordinary services. But this education of the negro, which fits him for the highest offices in the land, renders him a useless and discontented citizen. The whites cannot submit to negro rule and self-assertion. With the negroes equally distributed over the Union, this could be easily avoided. But so long as they remain with equal citizenship in the South they will continue a burden to themselves and to the white population. The South will remain the "Solid South" and prefer exclusion from national offices rather than allow the State offices to fall into the hands of negroes.

For this reason the colonization of the negro beyond the limits of the United States has ever found many supporters in Virginia as well as elsewhere. Mr. Monroe, who was the strong exponent of the Virginia sentiment for emancipation, said that he would never consent to the freedom of the slaves unless they were moved beyond the

THE SOUTHAMPTON INSURRECTION. 191

limits of this country. President Lincoln also agitated the question of colonizing the negro, and it would appear from his messages that he intended this as a sequel to the emancipation proclamation. In accordance with this, his recommendation made appropriations for this purpose. After the war many negroes petitioned Congress to aid them to migrate to Liberia.[1] But this spirit has died out and the negroes are becoming more organized. The state of affairs in Cuba forecasts a repetition of the scenes of 1831, only in a more pronounced form. Quintin Baudera, a negro general of prominence in the eastern province, has decided to found in Santiago a newspaper organ devoted to promoting the political interests of the negro military element, while Juan Guilberto Gomez, the ablest and most aggressive of the negro politicians of Cuba, has publicly severed his connection with the so-called National party and announced that he will head a new organization recruited chiefly from the negro officers and privates, who, it is claimed, bore the burden of insurrection against Spain. Such a claim will undoubtedly be made by the negro soldiers in the service of the United States. In this state of affairs the future is more to be feared than the present, and we have the same problem before us that confronts South Africa. Mr. Bryce's words are equally applicable to the Southern States of America. "No traveler," he says, "can study the color problem in South Africa without anxiety—anxiety not for the present, but for the future, in which the seeds that are now being sown will have sprung up and grown to maturity."[2] A careful consideration of present conditions in comparison with the history of slave insurrections leads to the conclusion that the colonization of the negro beyond the limits of the United States is the only means by which

[1] Sixty-second Annual Report of the American Colonization Society, in 1879.
[2] Impressions of South Africa, Chapter XXI.

hostility, strife, and insurrection can be avoided. In conclusion, the following considerations may be submitted:

First. The possibility and danger of negro insurrection are largely responsible for the suppression of the slave trade[1] and the substitution of negro slavery for negro servitude. The negroes at first enjoyed the same rights and privileges as the white indented servants,[2] with the exception of the possibility of social distinction and amalgamation with the white inhabitants. The Indians, English, French, and native whites of bad character took advantage of these facts to stir up discontent among the servants as well as the free negroes. Consequently, stringent legislation, which gradually led to the enslavement of the negro was necessary to put an end to such evils.[3]

Second. The condition of slavery in Virginia was not such as to arouse insurrections among the slaves. An affection existed between master and slave which has been handed down to their descendants, which dispelled that physical aversion and incompatibility of character and temper of the superior race for the inferior, stopped internecine wars, and prevented the general tendency of civilization to gradually blot out the inferior race. By this means alone has the perpetuity of the negro race been assured. Not one insurrection was due to cruel treatment or inbred desire for freedom.

Third. Superstition, religious fanaticism, and love of plunder and pillage have played a part in every slave insurrection in Virginia. Delusion has always been active. The weak and cowardly have participated, while the brave and intelligent slaves, in general, remained loyal.

Fourth. French and English intrigues, especially the

[1] DuBois, Suppression of the Slave Trade.
[2] Ballagh, White Servitude in Virginia.
[3] Proof of this will be more clearly seen in a work on "Slave Insurrections in Virginia from 1619 to 1830," which I hope to bring out within a year.

latter, have, from the earliest colonial period, exerted a powerful influence over the slaves of Virginia. Sierra Leone, on the west coast of Africa, was settled by negroes who fought on the British side in the War of Independence.

Fifth. The contiguity of three large bodies of free negroes—those of the West Indies, of South America, and of the Northern States and Canada—tended to incite the slaves of the South and to convince the people that the days of slavery were numbered.

Sixth. The Indian troubles not only incited the slaves to rebellion, but aroused in those sections more remote a sympathy for the negro which bore evil fruit.

Seventh. No slave insurrection would have occurred in Virginia but for the abolition movement in other sections.[1] On the contrary, the emancipation sentiment in Virginia would ultimately have led to the freedom of the slave and his colonization in Liberia. This example would have been followed by other Southern States. What Virginia and the South feared was not emancipation, but fanaticism. Self-preservation, the first law of nature, was the basic principle in the origin as well as in the continuance of negro slavery in Virginia.

Eighth. The slave legislation of Virginia was efficient and mild. It rendered the success of slave insurrection impossible, and laid the foundation of a training which rendered the negro a good and worthy citizen.

Ninth. Servile insurrections delayed the emancipation of the slaves in the United States. The emancipation sentiment was strong in the South as well as in the North,

---

[1] It was for this reason that the negroes were more closely guarded. Thus certificates were required from master or overseer for certain privileges and the slaves required to be in their quarters by a certain time. The citizens of Fayetteville, North Carolina, renewed the old custom of ringing "curfew" at 9 o'clock p. m., at which time all negroes were required to be in their quarter of the town. The custom is still in vogue there.

but abolition without colonization beyond the limits of the United States was advocated by few. Abolition was a war measure rather than the result of unanimity of Northern sentiment therefor.

Tenth. The negro, conscious of his inferiority, and equally distributed over the country, will make a peaceful and useful citizen. But educated for the highest offices, which he can never fill, he will remain a source of disturbance and insurrection, and under such circumstances it will be best for both races that the negro be transported beyond the limits of the United States.

END.

APPENDIX.

Appendix A.

A list of negroes brought before the court of Southampton, with their owners' names and sentences:[1]

Negroes.	Owner.	Sentence.
Daniel	Richard Porter	Convicted
Moses	J. T. Barrow	Convicted
Tom	Caty Whitehead	Discharged
Jack and Andrew	Caty Whitehead	Con. and transp't'd
Jacob	Geo. H. Charlton	Dis. without trial
Isaac	Geo. H. Charlton	Con. and trans.
Jack	Everett Bryant	Discharged
Nathan	Benj. Blunt's estate	Convicted
Nathan, Tom and Davy (boys)	Nathaniel Francis	Con. and trans.
Davy	Elizabeth Turner	Convicted
Curtis	Thomas Ridley	Convicted
Stephen	Thomas Ridley	Convicted
Hardy and Isham	Benj. Edwards	Con. and trans.
Sam	Nathaniel Francis	Convicted
Hark	Joseph Travis' estate	Convicted
Moses (a boy)	Joseph Travis' estate	Con. and trans.
Davy	Levi Waller	Convicted
Nelson	Jacob Williams	Convicted
Nat	Edmund Turner's estate	Convicted
Jack	Wm. Reese's estate	Convicted
Dred	Nathaniel Francis	Convicted
Arnold Artist (free)		Discharged
Sam	J. W. Parker	Acquitted
Ferry and Archer	J. W. Parker	Dis. without trial
Jim	Wm. Vaughan	Acquitted
Bob	Temperance Parker	Acquitted
Davy	Joseph Parker	
Daniel	Solomon D. Parker	Dis. without trial
Joe	John C. Turner	Convicted
Thos. Haithcock (free)		Sent for further trial

[1]Taken from Gray's "Confession of Nat Turner" and verified by comparison with county records.

APPENDIX.

Negroes.	Owner.	Sentence.
Lucy	John T. Barrow	Convicted
Matt	Thos. Ridley	Acquitted
Jim	Richard Porter	Acquitted
Exum Artes (free)		Sent for further trial
Joe	Richard P. Briggs	Dis. without trial
Berry Newsom (free)		Sent for further trial
Stephen	James Bell	Acquitted
Jim and Isaac	Samuel Champion	Con. and trans.
Preston	Hannah Williamson	Acquitted
Frank	Solomon D. Parker	Con. and trans.
Jack and Shadrack	Nathaniel Simmons	Acquitted
Nelson	Benj. Blunt's estate	Acquitted
Sam	Peter Edwards	Convicted
Archer	Arthur G. Reese	Acquitted
Isham Turner (free)		Sent for further trial
Nat Turner	Putnam Moore, deceased	Convicted

Appendix B.

LIST OF WHITE PERSONS MURDERED IN THE INSURRECTION.

Joseph Travis, his wife, Mrs. Sallie Travis, and one child; Putnam Moore, Joel Westbrook; Mrs. Elizabeth Turner, Hartwell Publes, Sarah Newsom; Mrs. P. Reese and her son, William Reese; Trajan Doyle; Henry Bryant, wife, child, and wife's mother; Mrs. Catherine Whitehead, her son, Richard, four daughters and a grandchild; Salathiel Francis; Mr. Nathaniel Francis' overseer, Mr. Henry Doyle, two nephews of Mr. N. Francis, named Brown; John T. Barrow, George Vaughan; Mrs. Levi Waller, her baby, Martha Waller, and Lucinda Jones and eight other school children; Mr. William Williams and wife; Miles and Henry Johnson; Mrs. Caswell Worrell and child; Mrs. Rebecca Vaughan, her son, Arthur, and her niece, Miss Anne Eliza Vaughan; Mrs. John K. Williams and child; Mrs. Jacob Williams and three children, and Mr. Edwin Drewry.

The above is the list as given by Mr. Thomas R. Gray in "The Confession, Trial, and Execution of Nat Turner." I have added the names of these persons wherever possible. There were other persons killed for whom it was impossible to account. Mr. Gray omits the overseer killed at Mrs. Rebecca Vaughan's. Some also say that fifteen persons, instead of eleven, were killed at Waller's.

APPENDIX.

Appendix C.

PRINCIPAL CITIZENS INTERVIEWED PERSONALLY.

a. Those living at the time of the Southampton insurrection:

Collin Kitchen (born 1806), Bowers, Va.
Mason Ryland (colored, born 1800), Brancheville, Va.
Miss Judith Thomas (born 1810), Newsoms, Va.
Sily Drake (born 1812), Pope, Va.
Miss Fanny Thomas (1820, circa), Newsoms, Va.
W. O. Denegre (born 1824), St. Paul, Minn.
James E. Westbrook, Sr. (born 1820), Drewryville, Va.
Capt. J. J. Darden (1824), Newsoms, Va
Robert W. Screws (born 1824), Newsoms, Va.
Benjamin Carter Everett (born 1818), Cooper's Store, Va.
Mrs. Charity Taylor (born 1816), Garysburg, N. C.
Hardie Musgrave (colored, born 1818), Newsoms, Va.
Bowlin Bass (born 1820), Adams Grove, Va.
Richard Hardin (colored, born 1810), Adams Grove, Va.
Mrs. Rebecca Francis (born 1820), Koskoo, Va.
Ann Jones Sykes (colored, born 1820), Boykins, Va.
Mrs. Vaughan (born 1821), Murfreesboro, N. C.
Mrs. Nancy Barker (1818), Seaboard, N. C.
Mrs. Rebecca Hart (born 1825), Turner's Cross Roads, N. C.
Mrs. Martha Jones (born 1827), Boykins, Va.
Mrs. Lavinia Francis (born 1810), Boykins, Va.
Col. David Hardee, Rehoboth, N. C.
Mrs. James Barnes (born 1824), Koskoo, Va.
Evelyn Jones (colored, born 1821), Drewryville, Va.
Edwin Williams, Courtland, Va.
Mrs. Wheeler, Seaboard, N. C.
Harry Clements (colored, born 1812, circa), Drewryville, Va.
Daniel Chapman (colored, born 1828, circa), Capron, Va.
Robert Mason (colored, born 1825), Brancheville, Va.
Benjamin Jones (colored, born 1820), Drewryville, Va.

b. Members of families which suffered from the insurrection, but born since that event:

W. S. Francis (born 1831), Brancheville, Va.
Miss Bettie Francis, Norfolk, Va.
Mrs. Caroline W. Stephenson, Seaboard, N. C.
B. F. McLemore, Courtland, Va.
James E. Westbrook, Jr., Drewryville, Va.
Mrs. Charles Nicholson, Assamoosick, Va.
Miss Mary Turner, Boykins, Va.
Mrs. J. J. Darden, Newsoms, Va.
Mrs. Frank Williams, Courtland, Va.
Burrell J. Wall, Garysburg, N. C.
Mrs. Lucinda Hill, Garysburg, N. C.

198   APPENDIX.

Mrs. John Dyer, Sunbeam, Va.
Miss Freddie Parker, Franklin, Va.
Mrs. Martha Drewry, Boykins, Va.
Mr. James Barmer, Seaboard, N. C.
William E. Leigh, Koskoo, Va.
Mrs. James D. Bryant, Franklin, Va.
J. F. DeBerry, Suffolk, Va.
Dr. W. F. Drewry, Petersburg, Va.
W. H. Drewry, Drewryville, Va.

c. Other persons who have had advantages for gaining original material relating to the massacre:

Dr. W. H. Daughtry, Sunbeam, Va.
R. S. Barham, Rehoboth, N. C.
Capt. James Barnes, Koskoo, Va.
Miss Martha Livesy, Boykins, Va.
Mrs. Bettie Moss, Boykins, Va.
Dr. Joseph Sykes, Boykins, Va.
J. L. Bishop, Newsoms, Va.
Judge J. B. Prince, Courtland, Va.
F. P. Brent, Richmond, Va.
J. Denson Pretlow, Courtland, Va.
Miss Julia Pretlow, Courtland, Va.
R. A. Brock, sec. Southern Historical Society, Richmond, Va.
W. G. Stannard, sec. Historical Society, Richmond, Va.
James D. Denegre, St. Paul, Minn.
Capt. W. H. Hood, Henderson, N. C.
Dr. John Eldridge, Murfreesboro, N. C.
J. S. Musgrave, Drewryville, Va.
John Sebrelle, Courtland, Va.
Solomon Wells (colored), Drewryville, Va.
Rosa Jones (colored), Drewryville, Va.
W. S. Clements (colored), Drewryville, Va.
Many others whom it is impossible to mention.
Letters from various citizens.

Appendix D.

BIBLIOGRAPHY.

a. Contemporaneous materials in Newspapers and Magazines:
The Norfolk Herald.
The Norfolk Beacon.
The Richmond Whig.
The Richmond Enquirer.
The Richmond Recorder.
The Richmond Intelligencer.
The Richmond Gazette.
The National Gazette.

APPENDIX.

The Boston Gazette (1800).
The Annual Register.
Niles Register.
Gentlemen's Magazine.
Virginia Magazine of History and Biography.
The Genius of Universal Emancipation.
American Annual Register.

b. Pamphlets:
Confession, Trial and Execution of Nat Turner. By Thomas Gray.
Trial and Executions of the Negro Conspirators of Charleston, S. C., 1822.
Trial and Imprisonment of Jonathan Walker at Pensacola, Fla.
"The Slaves" (Written for the Commencement of 1831 of the Western Reserve College, by James B. Walker.)
Speech of Hon. Percy Walker, of Alabama.
Walker's Appeal.
Slavery in Rebellion (anonymous).
Slave Insurrections. Joshua Coffin.
Birney Collection of Pamphlets on Slavery (including reports, proceedings, etc., of the African Colonization and Anti-Slavery Societies).

c. Magazines and papers of later date.
Richmond Dispatch.
The Macon Telegraph.
The Patron and Gleaner, of Rich Square, N. C.
The Nat Turner Insurrection. W. H. Parker.
Ephraim's Light in Wake Forest Student.
Godey's Magazine (March, 1898).

d. Legal Documents, Proceedings, and Laws:
Calendar of Virginia State Papers.
Acts of the Virginia Assembly.
Journal of House of Delegates.
Journal of Virginia Senate.
Journal of House of Burgesses.
Hening. Statutes.
J. C. Hurd. Law of Freedom and Bondage.
Hening. Justice.
Shroud. Sketch of the Laws of Slavery.
S. B. Weeks. Negro Suffrage in the South.
Court Records of Southampton County.
Saintsbury MSS.
Spotswood Letters.
Dinwiddie Papers.
Letters to the Governors of Virginia.
Petitions to Virginia Legislature.
Macdonald. Select Documents of United States History.
Richardson. Messages and Papers of the Presidents.

Made in the USA
Columbia, SC
22 September 2017